WHEN BROOKLYN
WAS THE WORLD

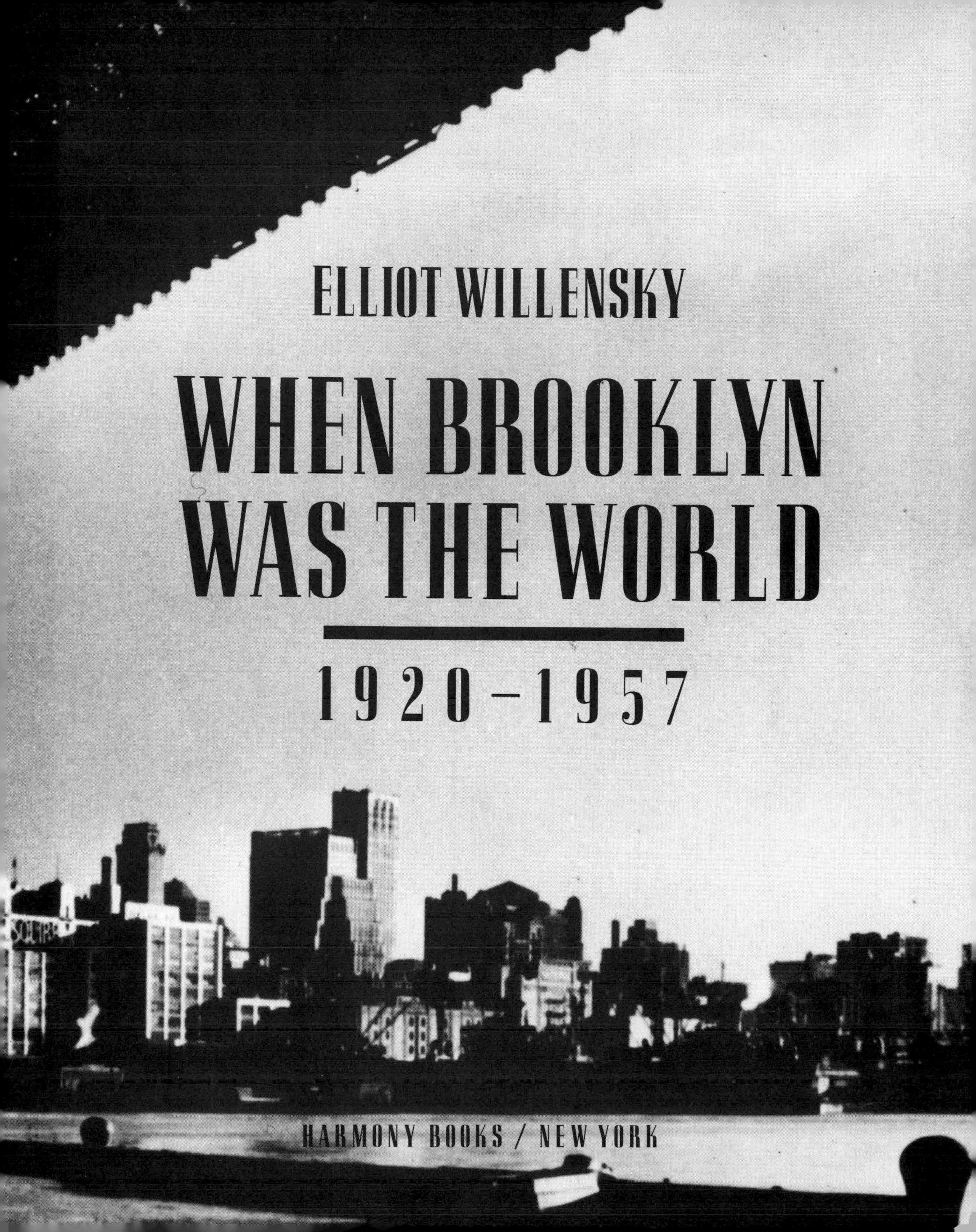

ELLIOT WILLENSKY

WHEN BROOKLYN WAS THE WORLD

1920–1957

HARMONY BOOKS / NEW YORK

BOOKS BY ELLIOT WILLENSKY

The A.I.A. Guide to New York City
(with Norval White)

An Urban Information System for New York City

Guide to Developing a Neighborhood Marker System

Published by Harmony Books, a division of Crown Publishers, Inc.
201 East 50th Street,
New York, New York 10022

HARMONY and colophon are trademarks of Crown Publishers, Inc.

Manufactured in the United States of America

Library of Congress Cataloging-in-Publication Data

Willensky, Elliot.
When Brooklyn was the world, 1920–1957.

1. Brooklyn (New York, N.Y.)—History.   2. Brooklyn (New York, N.Y.)—Social life
and customs.   3. New York (N.Y.)—History.   4. New York (N.Y.)—Social life and
customs.   5. Brooklyn (New York, N.Y.)—Description—Views.   6. New York (N.Y.)
—Description—Views.   I. Title. F129.B7W58   1986   974.7'23   85-5482
ISBN 0-517-55858-0

10 9 8 7 6 5

To
Fannie Eisenstein Willensky
who, with my late father Morris, started me on all this

Margaret Webb Latimer
who encouraged me unflaggingly

Philip Chaitovitch Ressner
who was both my conscience and my guide

Marc Isaac Willensky and Diana Gwen Willensky
who seem intent on continuing the journey

Hot dogs from Nedicks's "Orange Room," dress suits to hire "from upstairs," and grimy monkey wrenches from Sam's Hardware "next door" combined with photoplays, radio parts, and evidence of a vast trolley car empire to make a Brooklyn that is no more. This spot, at Washington Street and Myrtle Avenue, now lies practically under the State Supreme Court building.

CONTENTS

ACKNOWLEDGMENTS

I am grateful that so many people were eager to share with me their memories of life in Brooklyn during the period explored in this book. It is perhaps because I value the visual form of a place as an important clue to the events that have taken place there that I especially appreciated the personally guided tours of the Brooklyn neighborhoods of their youth taken in the company of Victor Bach, Michael George, Philip Ressner, Carole Rifkind and Marilyn Berger, and Howard Morhaim. Many of their evocative recollections will remain with me for a long time. Jay and Rosalee Harris enthusiastically shared vivid, amusing, and touching accounts of their relatively brief stay in Brooklyn. Lenora LaRocca Brennan was kind enough to tape a walk through her old neighborhood with Margaret Latimer, which proved to be very helpful. Others re-created the richness of their Brooklyn experiences in words: in particular William Alex, Irving Choban, and Joseph De Simone—who introduced me to a slice of life in Brooklyn with which I was totally unfamiliar. He also permitted me to look through personal family photo albums, whose unlabeled snapshots of the twenties, thirties, and forties he verbally captioned in a very loving way.

Others offered photographic materials from their family albums that also proved very useful: Alan Haber, Lenora Brennan, and Lorna Nowve. Dianne Esses, coordinator of the Sephardic Archives, acted as intermediary to obtain access to a number of snapshots from people such as Anita Garner and Beatrice Serure, whom I don't know personally. Messrs. Bedi and Makky, former and current owners of the Bedi-Makky Art Foundry, were helpful with clippings and photos of the Iwo Jima statue cast in the foundry. Russell Gilmore, director of the Harbor Defense Museum at Fort Hamilton, was extremely supportive in alerting me to sources of World War II military photographs, particularly at the Defense Audio Visual Agency's Washington Activity. Esther Brumberg aided in identifying sources of other visual materials.

David M. Kahn, Executive Director of what was then known as the Long Island Historical Society and now bears the name Brooklyn Historical Society, was unusually attentive to my needs at his institution, and its librarian Lucinda Manning and others of the staff extended themselves to accommodate me during my research phase. Gunther Pohl, chief of the New York Public Library's Local History and Genealogy Division, now retired, helped make the photographic collections in his charge even more valuable research tools. Tom Knight, Brooklyn's official Baseball Historian, was ever ready to clarify the sticky questions I had about the Dodgers. Elizabeth White and the photographs in the Brooklyn Collection of the Brooklyn Public Library made the task of compiling the necessary illustrative material easier.

Others, though not Brooklynites, contributed ideas, suggestions, and comments that made my task more intriguing and enjoyable: Gretchen Duchac, Sue Radmer, John Tauranac, Warren Wechsler, Kent Barwick, Lew Davis, and Bob Bien.

Special recognition is due to the unsung individuals of the Brooklyn Public Library Telephone Reference Service for their good-humored cooperation in accurately resolving difficult last-minute factual questions about Brooklyn.

When my writing task was largely completed, my friend Phil Ressner, after long days at his daytime editing job, reworked the entire manuscript as only a superb editor could. He and other friends, Vic Bach, Bill Alex, Howard Morhaim, and Peggy Latimer, read the finished manuscript and offered important suggestions for improvement and clarification, not all of which, I regret, was I able to incorporate.

Publisher Bruce Harris, himself a native of Brooklyn, editor Harriet Bell, designer Ken Sansone, and editorial director Esther Mitgang contributed every ounce of their talents and skills to this effort.

Though already acknowledged above, Margaret W. Latimer's ready assistance and encouragement in so many different ways, including the use of superb materials developed through her Brooklyn Rediscovery program, were an invaluable asset to me.

Once people are aware that you're writing a book about Brooklyn, there appears an outpouring of generosity that I believe would be unmatched for just about any other subject. I am certain, therefore, that I have left out the names of many people who were also helpful to me in this project; to them I extend my deepest apologies. To both those I have acknowledged here and to those unnamed others, thank you all for your contributions, your assistance, and your encouragement.

INTRODUCTION

ow do you sort out a vision of the place you once called home?—particularly since published accounts and personal memories rarely coincide.

How much of what is remembered is fact, how much fantasy? Which of these contributes more to making quiet those dancing memories, so vivid yet so distant, of a time long gone and a place so changed? And what of those other nearby places that beckoned, just out of reach, that were strange then and perhaps remain unfamiliar even now? Around the corner. The next block. Across the tracks. At the end of the line. Borough Park. Gowanus. Flatbush. Canarsie. Ridgewood. Greenpoint. Brownsville. Bay Ridge. Bensonhurst. City Line. Which ones did you live in? Which ones beckoned?

When all of these places, and more, were part of a collective identity, one that you either accepted proudly—or just couldn't easily escape—that collective identity called Brooklyn, then what? What was that place called Brooklyn really like back then, when you were growing up?

For Brooklyn, the years 1920 through 1957 represent a kind of golden age. It was in 1920 that subway system branches reached into New Lots and Flatbush, and express lines—the Brighton, Sea Beach, West End, and Culver—finally linked Manhattan with Brooklyn's extreme edge, the oceanfront at Coney Island. New trains crisscrossed the flat landscape on shining rails and provided the ease of access that was instrumental in establishing a swarm of residential communities across the width and breadth of the borough. In both 1922 and 1923, Brooklyn—actually Kings County—led the nation's counties in housing construction.

Gridlock for Brooklyn began in the 1930s at Fourth Avenue's intersection with Atlantic and Flatbush avenues. Belt Parkway had not yet been completed to give drivers a circumferential route.

As 1920 marked a beginning, the 1950s marked an end. The year 1957 was to be the last that Brooklyn's beloved Dodgers would occupy Ebbets Field. Since 1884 the annual struggle of the Brooklyn baseball team to defeat its foes had touched the hearts of Brooklynites. The fate of the home team represented to many the fate of Brooklyn. Finally, in 1955, after decades of defeat (and years after first receiving the label "Dem Bums"), the team not only captured the National League pennant but won the coveted World Series as well, vanquishing the heroic Yankees, yet! For Brooklyn fans it was a repeat of V-J Day. But the elation was to be very, very brief. Brooklynites had at last fulfilled their promised destiny, only to lose it again with wrenching finality. Two years after their Series victory, in 1957, the Dodgers' management, under president Walter O'Malley (boo! hiss!), took the team across the continent to Chavez Ravine. (And if that was not enough, the monument that was Ebbets Field was shortly to be demolished, for high-rise housing, no less.)

The years between 1920 and the Dodgers' departure were rich in events and images for Brooklyn. They were the years of Luna Park and Steeplechase, Coney Island's (the world's?) great amusement centers. They were the years in which great ethnic communities arose, flourished, left their distinctive marks upon the cityscape, and sent their sons and daughters out into the larger world. They were the years of boom and of depression, years in which the boundaries of Brooklyn became girdled with the amber-lit Belt Parkway, when the mucky edges of a tidal inlet called Sheepshead Bay were rebuilt into a fisherman's paradise through the largesse of the WPA and the federal Public Works Administration, whose dollars also built Brooklyn a college of its own that proudly bears its name.

Those years were the years when the phrase "before (or after) the war" referred to World War II. World War I was the conflict

The automobile was already a way of life when these detached houses near Avenue M and Twenty-first Street were built. The driveway and separate garage became a necessary part of every builder's vocabulary.

The presidential election of 1936 was only a few days away when President Franklin Delano Roosevelt paid a visit to heavily Democratic Brooklyn to participate in the cornerstone-laying ceremony at Brooklyn College. Appearing humbled by the occasion was his friend Fiorello H. LaGuardia, who would be seeking a second term as mayor the next year.

that gave us men in American Legion uniforms and VFW outfits and women in nurses' caps, whose presence in parades lent a patriotic spirit to our lives. The First World War, for us, wasn't *the* war, *our* war. And neither was Korea, whose label "police action" still rings false in our ears.

This, then, is a book of recollections about Brooklyn before the war, during the war, and after the war. I hope they ring true; more important, I hope they enable you—whether or not you lived in Brooklyn in those years—to summon up your own memories of the past, the ones that for you are the most meaningful.

E.W.

Daily News editors couldn't contain themselves. The Dodgers had won the 1955 World Series, and Leo O'Melia's memorable cartoon made it to the paper's front page.

1

ARE YOU REALLY FROM BROOKLYN?

hat's so special about being from Brooklyn? Why the envy? Why the wonder? Why the grin?

For years now, a Brooklyn background has carried with it a special standing. It hasn't always been a totally flattering one. There was a time when merely the mention of the name Brooklyn would evoke a snicker, in some cases even a guffaw. Brooklyn has been the butt of jokes in bars, on radio and TV, in Borscht Belt resorts, in cartoons and headlines. Every nickel-and-dime comic could be sure of a laugh by just mentioning Flatbush or Brighton Beach or Canarsie. Sometimes it was a laugh of recognition, other times of derision. In the 1940s, Hollywood had a field day with Brooklyn. Hardly a film was made about the war that didn't feature at least one cocky draftee with an ethnic moniker talking in a working-class dialect, chewing gum, and grubbing cigarettes. Invariably, when he announced his hometown—with pride—it was Brooklyn. Laughter.

Things got so bad just before World War II that a Brooklynite named Sid Ascher and some friends formed the Society for the Prevention of Disparaging Remarks Against Brooklyn as a gag. But by 1946 it claimed forty thousand members who, during that year alone, tallied three thousand slanders of Brooklyn in the media.

In 1936 the Roosevelt administration, experiencing a large number of court challenges to its controversial National Recovery Administration—remember the NRA blue eagle in practically every store window?—chose to take the appeal from a live poultry

Rooftop signs label many of downtown Brooklyn's buildings viewed from the top of the Williamsburgh Savings Bank tower, newly opened in 1929. The Fifth Avenue elevated can be seen along Flatbush Avenue while the other set of tracks marks the path of Fulton Street's el.

Every ethnic group had its benevolent society. This one, Societa Di San Giovanni Battista, is shown at its annual parade in 1922 on President Street between Third Avenue and Nevins Street.

dealer at 858 East Fifty-second Street in Brooklyn (of all places) to the Supreme Court. The case, remembered in the history books as *Schechter Poultry Corporation, Schechter Live Poultry Market, Joseph Schechter, Martin Schechter, Alex Schechter, and Aaron Schechter vs. The United States of America,* turned out to be the downfall of the NRA when the court unanimously found the legislation unconstitutional. Predictably, it also turned out to be a special experience for the court, for Joseph Schechter's graphic recitation of the techniques of chicken slaughter, according to *The New York Times,* "sent the usually solemn justices into gales of laughter." And although the Schechter brothers won their case, they complained bitterly that the $22,000 in lawyer's fees cost them their every nickel. Mrs. Joseph Schechter's feelings later

found their way into a poem entitled "Now That It's Over":

> No more excuses
>   To hide our disgrace;
> With pride and satisfaction
>   I'm showing my face.
>
> For a long, long time
>   To be kept in suspense,
> Sarcastic remarks made
>   At our expense.
>
> I'm through with that experience
>   I hope for all my life
> And proud again to be
>   Joseph Schechter's wife.

Downtown Brooklyn was a busy place between the wars. But close by were slums not too different from those Eleanor Roosevelt complained about near the Capitol in Washington. Is that an outhouse we see in the lower right of the picture?

The origins of Alfred E. Neuman, *Mad Comic*'s "What—Me Worry" boy, are cloudy. A contender may be this "It Didn't Hurt a Bit" sign at Flatbush and Third avenues, at Temple Square. The building was demolished just before 1920 to sink the 500-foot-deep Shaft 23 for a new city water tunnel.

Part of one's identification with Brooklyn came from the way others saw you, and that was often with a touch of wry amusement. But another part came from how you saw yourself, and saw that special place you called home.

Snobbery was part of it. Big, klutzy Brooklyn always seemed to wind up playing second fiddle to svelte Manhattan. Even though Brooklyn was an independent city until 1898—America's third largest, at that—its proximity to Manhattan, its wide-open spaces, and its growing role as an enormous bedroom community for Manhattan's workers made it a perfect target for derision. It's not that the place was totally filled with the country-bumpkin cousins of snooty Manhattanites. Brooklyn had its own blue bloods, a proud aristocracy that traced its family names back to Brooklyn's beginnings. Local street signs certainly bore testament to that: Remsen, Livingston, Ditmas, Cortelyou. But the old families were Brooklyn's minority. The more abundant of its people, particularly after the population explosion of the 1920s, were its newcomers, those of more modest means looking to make a better life. They had, for the most part, relocated from poorer, less desirable places in Brooklyn, Manhattan, and elsewhere to find an affordable spot to raise a family, often in an apartment. In the minds of Manhattan's tastemakers, however, they had moved to the provinces. And who lives in the provinces? Why, provincials do, of course. Brooklynites do.

Living in Brooklyn in those days meant, for most, either living within the working class or marginally achieving middle-class respectability. Given the borough's economic profile, it was hardly possible for most Brooklynites to marry *beneath* their station, unless you meant one on the el.

To make good was an important objective for many, and judging merely from the list of show business personalities with Brooklyn roots, many did: Mickey Rooney, Jackie Gleason, George Gershwin, Moss Hart, Lena Horne, Barbara Stanwyck, Phil Silvers, Marion Davies, Irving Thalberg, Danny Kaye, Helen Gahagen Douglas, Sam Levenson, Abe Burrows, Shelley Winters, Barbra Streisand, Buddy Hackett, Mary Tyler Moore, Woody Allen. Lists from other professions would be equally long. Longer, even.

Lindsay Park playground was a popular spot for Williamsburg kids in the summer of 1929. The super blocks of the project called Lindsay Park Houses now occupy the area.

That desire—to make good—branded Brooklynites as upstarts in the minds of the successful, and strivers among the less so. They were so easy to identify. You had only to listen to the way most of them spoke English. It was really no surprise that so many used the distinctive vernacular branded "Brooklynese," even though its jarring mispronunciations, ostentatious dentalizations, and curious inflections were by no means limited only to Brooklyn. The parents and grandparents of most of those with provincial pronunciation were often first-generation Americans, many not long off the boat. Those from Ireland or England spoke a heavily accented English, but English nevertheless. Most spoke no English at all, but gained a fractured version somewhere on the Lower East Side, Hell's Kitchen, or Hoboken. How else would you learn the native tongue but from your second-generation schoolteachers—who, in those years, often bore Irish surnames? Or from those folks on your block who might have been around just a bit longer than yours. And who exactly had taught *them* the language? Surely not the blue bloods.

Some of the newcomers accepted the unfamiliar sounds uncritically and proceeded to teach them, in turn, to *their* children. Others recognized the limitations of the patois and assumed a set of snootier—but often just as inappropriate—usages and pronunciations: "Just between you and I . . . " That group ran the risk of being called "stuck up." Rightfully so.

Gravesend Bay was still lined with piers and beachfront facilities in the early twenties, and boys would swim in it regardless of the threat of pollution. The Captain's Pier, in Bath Beach, shown here on a quiet weekday, was a popular place.

The special ways they pronounced their vowels and consonants, or failed to, came to mark as Brooklynites—sometimes indelibly—those who learned to speak on the streets of Greenpernt, Bensonhoist, or Bvownsville:

Dem, dese, and dose. The substitution of *"erl"* for "oil" and *"oil"* for "earl." All the *r* variants, dropped as in "nevuh mind," added, as in "That's a great idear, " or replaced by a soft *v*, as in "He's vevy, vevy vich." These became common clichés about the speech of Brooklyn's people. And to ask (or "aks," as was more often the case) many a Brooklynite to pronounce "asterisk"—akstericks, askerisk, atserist—was only to provoke a shy, tolerant smile.

Mispronunciation was only one of the dialect's special qualities. Another was one of rhythm and emphasis. Commonly heard in Brooklyn's many Jewish neighborhoods was the Talmudic singsong that came with the need to make a trenchant point. It's a style most familiar today in the speech patterns of Mayor Edward Koch (himself, however, not a Brooklyn native). With so many *tatehs* and *mommehs* having come from little *shtetlakh,* how could they *not* have influenced their children's ways? Listen. After all. I ask you. So? (In the forties and fifties, Brooklyn College insisted that students take Speech as a required subject—as much as five courses, two and a half years, the number depending on the results of a speech test given at the time of admission.)

Was there also something about Brooklyn's ambience in those years that made it such a special place for its residents as well as for strangers? Did it have—actually have—a character all its own? Did out-of-the-ordinary things go on there? Was Brooklyn *really* unique? After all, a good commercial atlas will show more than three dozen Brooklyns, including one in Illinois that's an all-black community. There is even one in Nova Scotia; no, not in recognition of all that nova—mildly salted lox—reputedly consumed in Brooklyn, N.Y.

Brooklyn, N.Y., *is* special. When people ask "Are you really from Brooklyn?" you can be sure they know which one they're talking about. They mean *our* Brooklyn, the one on the southwest extremity of Long Island, or "Lon gIsland," as many natives still call it. They mean the *big* Brooklyn, the one with a population of millions, the one whose highway signs used to announce it as "America's Fourth Largest City." Brooklyn not only holds the title as the most populous of New York State's sixty-two counties and the city's five boroughs, but has held that distinction since the end

The Fourth of July, Armistice Day, or any other excuse for a get-together would bring families and neighbors into the backyard. Patriotic bunting would be hung, decorations put up, and kegs of beer ordered. But some little kids didn't really appreciate the fun.

Jackie "The Kid" Coogan is held aloft to the cheers of more than eighty-four thousand persons who voyaged to Prospect Park in the early twenties to greet the popular child star of silent films. In the front row are Brooklyn Edison Boy Scouts.

of the 1920s construction boom, when its newly gained population of 2.5 million pulled it far ahead of Manhattan's earlier record of 1.8.

In that period—between the onset of the twenties and the fifties—Brooklyn's size, population, and history did make it a special place, actually a special *combination* of places. Sure, it was a bedroom community for Manhattan. But it had lots of the hallmarks of a city unto itself, of a city it had actually and officially been, not too many years earlier. It had a downtown of its own, with big department stores, lavish theaters, splashy restaurants, tall office buildings; it had a bunch of spiffy hotels with rooftop restaurants and grand ballrooms; it had belts of industry and commerce that blackened the sky and filled the streets with smells of roasting coffee beans and aromatic teas and pungent spices offloaded from freighters from all parts of the globe. It had wetlands and marshes and artesian wells in waterworks of its own. It had a classy local newspaper, the *Brooklyn Eagle*—with a Paris office, yet—and it had a baseball team whose zany antics made it both a prize and an embarrassment.

But Brooklyn was vexed by an identity problem. Though officially deprived of its own municipal status at the turn of the century, was it still a city de facto? Or was it, as the legislation decreed, just a borough of America's largest city? Debating this question wasn't just a philosophical pastime; it revealed some of the dissonances in Brooklyn's self-image.

It also shed a sardonic light on its contrasts. Brooklyn enjoyed the verdancy of a great urban greensward, Prospect Park, labeled by its designers, Olmsted and Vaux, as their best effort—even better than their earlier Central Park in Manhattan. Yet it also suffered the stench of the Gowanus Canal, "Lavender Lake" to its hardened neighbors. On the other hand, Greenwood Cemetery, which had lost its nineteenth-century spelling "Green-Wood," was still a great treasury of Victorian memorials to monumental figures in Brooklyn's, New York's, and the nation's history. While Manhattan's considerable shoreline of the twenties was largely an industrial and commercial wasteland, Brooklyn's was a model of variety, encompassing not just warehouses and piers, but also shorefront roads, an array of beaches, and waterfront recreation spots at Coney Island, Bath and Bergen beaches, Brighton, Sea Gate, and Canarsie. Brooklyn boasted mile after mile of superbly ornamented, crafted, and preserved brownstone residences, revered once again today for their urbanity and beauty. Even Brooklyn's industry had character, had "grit." Yet to many who passed through, "monotonous" was not an inappropriate word for mile upon mile of Brooklyn's vast urban texture. Much of it is.

"Don't they know their place?" some asked. "Why do they call so much attention to Brooklyn (even when they don't mean to)?" But to others, the idea of Brooklyn was a welcome relief from the tedium of their lives. To that group it was a vicarious substitute for the deeper monotony of their own community, the place where they happened to live that simply didn't have the special character they believed was Brooklyn's. Ogden Nash quipped, "The Bronx. No thonks." And Queens? People who hailed from places like Flushing or Beechhurst or Garden Bay Manor regarded their communities—rather than the borough as a whole—with pride. They were never heard to boast, "I'm from Queens." And them from

In the silent era of films, even the marquees remained silent, offering no indication of what was playing. The Boro Park, displaying a commonly used abbreviation of the community name, stood at New Utrecht Avenue and Fifty-first Street, the site of today's Blythebourne Post Office Station.

Staten Island? They were really from the sticks. Whether they came from within its boundaries or without, lots of folks considered Brooklyn a latter-day Camelot.

When a place the size of Brooklyn finds itself overflowing with so many, many millions of men, women, and children, the density of that influx can also have a particularly powerful impact upon their lives. People are put in closer touch—literally—with one another. In some poorer households, children slept three to a bed. Among Brooklyn's Italian community there evolved this urban blessing: "May God protect you from bad neighbors and students of the violin."

Inevitably, life in many congested parts of Brooklyn spilled out onto the streets from the pre-forties walkups and elevator apartments and two- and four-family houses and from the little garden apartments and high-rise projects that were built after the inter-

A quiet scene during the forties of the area between Kings County Hospital and Holy Cross Cemetery, a neighborhood of neat detached homes, carefully trimmed hedges, and full-bodied trees looking healthy even in winter.

ruptions of the Depression and World War II. Come the summer, to escape the stifling heat, even the old folks would go "outside," to sit on the stoops, as if they were bleachers, or on folding chairs along the curb. In those days, before the window air conditioner, even cross-ventilation wouldn't erase the city's annual midyear discomfort: "It isn't the heat, Gertie, it's the humidity."

Pinochle. Dominoes. Pitch pennies. A card game called pisha paysha. Gin. For a time in the late forties and fifties the popular game was canasta. Brooklyn's own card expert, Oswald Jacoby, is credited with the comment, "After you've played your first game, your chief problem will be how to stop." The same could have been said of another pastime that caused Brooklyn's streets to resound: "Eight bam, call, three crak, east, seven dot, same, flower, soap, green . . . Mah-Jongg!" The ancient Chinese game had made inroads in a place where being Chinese was about as common as being from an old family. But unlike Brooklyn's aristocrats, the Chinese were dispersed, many of them in behind-the-store living quarters of the ubiquitous hand laundries that dotted Brooklyn's neighborhoods, and in the growing number of "chinks"—what the more abundant (and less discreet) minorities called Chinese restaurants.

When school was out, Brooklyn streets rang with the voices of mothers bellowing the names of their kids out of upper-floor windows. And what names they were: Anthony (Tony, Ants), or Michael (Mike, Mickey), Joseph (Joey, Yussy), or Harold (Harry, Hesh); and others like Marsha, Gail, Roseanne, or Marie. *Real* names they were, not names like today's Jason or Ethan, Stacey or Tiffany. Only public-school records showed the existence of pupils named Elliot; to family and to friends on the block they were Eli.

And why were they being summoned? "Where's your *sis*-tuh?" "Time for your milk and *crah*-kuhs" or "Bring me a bunch soup greens from the fruit store." Such latter messages were followed by the inevitable sign-off: "Catch!" At which point, down would plummet a tiny missile, a few coins wrapped in a scrap of paper, or a dollar bill weighted with a skate key doing double duty, having been forgotten "upstairs" in the after-school hassle to drop one's books and get quickly back "downstairs."

"And don't forget to bring back the *chay*-unge!"

In a few parts of Brooklyn this kind of street life was held in contempt; it barely existed. Stoops of Brooklyn Heights brownstones, for example, were meant for ascending or descending, certainly not for hanging out, Goodness Gracious! What did initiate consternation in that proud precinct were the seemingly incessant conversations between the harbor's salty tugboat captains and pilots of merchant ships, expressed by the toots and peeps of their whistles. Frequent letters of complaint to the local newspaper were impatient to the point of foot-tapping.

To a stranger, most of Brooklyn's sounds were of a noticeable stridency. Brooklyn was a noisy place. Practically everywhere, strings of elevated cars rattled overhead—downtown along Fulton Street, or even out in East New York, where they screeched their sinuous way into Broadway Junction's multileveled, steel-girdered ganglia. Day and night—it didn't matter that you were sleeping—police and ambulance sirens knifed through the traffic on Flatbush Avenue, Kings Highway, or Eastern Parkway. Was it your imagination, or did Brooklyn really have a disproportionately large number of emergencies?

On winter mornings it wasn't unusual to be awakened by the glittering scratch of a coal truck's black load sluicing down a metal chute into a cellar coal bin. And hardly a day passed without the bone-rattling chatter of pneumatic drills cutting into Brooklyn's pavements, especially during the Depression, when red-white-

and-blue WPA signs seemed everywhere, and men with shovels were not far behind. The din seemed never-ending.

Most Brooklynites lived inland, away from the miles and miles of river, bay, and oceanfront that ringed the borough. But for those who lived close to the water, or for those thousands of rush-hour straphangers who crossed the Brooklyn, Manhattan, or Williamsburg bridges, Brooklyn's water boundaries rarely failed to offer some intriguing sight: tugboats, scows, derricks, car floats, or sometimes a larger vessel, a stately passenger liner, a dreadnought steaming to the Navy Yard, or a freighter. (In those days, freighters were referred to as merchantmen, leading at least one landlocked youngster to assume that Brooklyn's fabled wharves were lined with a phalanx of maritime Paul Bunyans in giant hip boots.)

In the summertime it was the Atlantic Ocean and Brooklyn's beaches (which verged on it) that beckoned—particularly Coney

Maritime industries flourished along Brooklyn's shoreline. Here, at the Robins Plant of the Todd Shipyards Corporation in Erie Basin, the S.S. *Stockholm* rests in dry dock during overhaul.

Island, so near and so accessible. Many families rented so-called bungalows at the beach, where Momma would continue the drudgery of housekeeping but could look forward to the evening sea breezes to make the summer tolerable. Trips to the surf on weekdays could actually be refreshing; on weekends the crush of crowds concealed the sand. For those who didn't like sand, there were city-run swimming pools like Betsy Head, in Brownsville, or private ones like Farragut, in more middle-class areas; and the gush of open fire hydrants was a dependable last resort.

Others left Brooklyn to spend summer vacations in "the mountains," the Catskills, reached by long-distance bus (Brooklyn had its own bus terminals), shiny black limousine, or the overloaded family car. "Going to the country this year?" Practically every ethnic group had its part of the Catskills and its own nickname for it. To some it was the Borscht Belt, to others the German (or Italian) Alps. For those who didn't get to go to places like Loch

Despite the glories of Brooklyn's ocean beaches, some preferred familiar faces at the neighborhood swimming hole. Renting a season locker at the local pool and athletic club was a summertime tradition in some neighborhoods.

Sheldrake or East Durham or Fleischmanns or Cairo, it was either sleep-over camp (as distinguished from "day") or "tar beach," the impromptu recreation area amid the clotheslines on one's apartment-house roof. It was perfect for sunbathing or, on hot nights, for sleeping—if the mosquitoes didn't bother you or if you didn't mind applying oil of citronella. (Did *your* family use witch hazel for mosquito bites? Did it really help?)

Horsedrawn wagons were still a way of making deliveries in those days, and many an Italian family's backyard garden was fertilized with horse manure scooped up with a broad coal shovel soon after a wagon had passed. Automobiles were not really abundant until after World War II. So, for most Brooklynites, local travel usually meant a trolley car ride or an experimental "trackless trolley" or the subway called the BMT, the Brooklyn-Manhattan Transit. The older IRT (Interborough Rapid Transit), and the city's IND (Independent Subway System)—which only started to traverse Brooklyn in the thirties—didn't really count as much; they were more citywide in their routes and anyway, unlike the BMT, they didn't carry Brooklyn in their names.

While those who could afford it chose a summer respite in "The Mountains" or a bungalow at Brighton, Coney, or even Rockaway(!), some younger Brooklynites spent time at camps run by local charities.

NINTH AV.
CITY HALL
62ND ST. B'KLYN
BAY PARKWAY
CONEY ISLAND
TIMES SQUARE
KINGS HIGHWAY
57TH ST. MANH'T'N.
BRIGHTON BEACH
NASSAU ST.
FRANKLIN-NASSAU
FRANKLIN AV.
PROSPECT PARK
95TH ST. FT. H'TON.
QUEENS PLAZA
WHITEHALL ST.

Part of the destination sign rolled up in a typical BMT subway car of the period.

The BMT was special. Where but in Brooklyn, with its well-drained sandy soil, could so many of its subway lines have been placed in giant-sized, concrete-lined furrows open to the sky? Where but in Brooklyn would a rapid-transit system have electric signs and buzzers that announced the approach of trains so that passengers could huddle around the warmth of a pot belly coal stove near the change booth instead of waiting on a chilly platform? Forerunners of computer-controlled highway signs and the Transit Authority red beeping monsters, they buzzed and blinked TO CITY and TO CONEY ISLAND to announce the respective trains. And where but in Brooklyn would an otherwise impersonal transit system display a prim sign warning of unexpected surges of wind? WARNING—HOLD YOUR HAT, it said, where it hung at the end of the underwater tunnel in Brooklyn Heights' breezy Court Street station.

Until 1959, when it was extended to embrace Queens (We wuz robbed!), Brooklyn even had a holiday all its own. On the first Thursday in June, all its public-school pupils got an extra day off. It was called Brooklyn (or Anniversary) Day, and over the years fewer and fewer knew—or cared—why it was celebrated. Every year it appeared again, somehow to everyone's surprise and delight. It seemed as if one were getting something for nothing, and so the fewer questions asked, the better. Actually, the date marked the creation, in 1829, of the Brooklyn Sunday School Union, a Protestant group. It was the cause for joyous parades that for years were very popular events, which still occur in a much-reduced form, largely within the black community that accounts for many of the borough's Protestants.

As special as Brooklyn was in those years, there still were those who felt that it needed something special to strengthen its identity even further—an image of purity and gaiety—perhaps a flower. A yellow flower. A yellow spring flower. It was in 1940 that Mrs. Edward C. Blum, wife of the president of the Abraham & Straus department store, and member of the Brooklyn Botanic Garden's Women's Auxiliary, persuaded then Borough President John Cashmore to declare the forsythia Brooklyn's official bloom. It was unclear whether this was to counter the effect upon the borough's image of the prolific ailanthus—the tree (some say giant weed) made famous in Betty Smith's novel, *A Tree Grows in Brooklyn,* or whether it was meant as a gracious act of boosterism in its own right. In any case, the forsythia still prevails.

The image that Brooklynites most revered during this period

was, as it turned out, neither a flower nor a tree. It was that of their own zany, tragicomic baseball team, familiarly known to all aficionados of sport as "the Flock." From its beginnings in the nineteenth century, Brooklyn's National League ball team had gone through a number of name changes. At first it was dryly referred to simply as "Brooklyn." At a time when many on the team were married, the handle "Bridegrooms" emerged, and they were even called the Superbas for a time, after a popular musical. In the 1890s, with Brooklynites scooting to get out of the way of all those newfangled electric trolleys that were replacing the horsecars, the nickname "Trolley Dodgers" became popular, soon abbreviated to "Dodgers." Later it was changed to the Robins, after manager (between 1914 and 1931) Wilbert Robinson. Then, following a brief flirtation with the name Brooklyn Kings—after the county congruent with the borough—the old name was reinstated again, and Dodgers they remain to this day, but, alas, no longer in Brooklyn.

What made the players dear to the hearts of just about everyone in the borough was their amazing ability to pull off the unexpected, far more often than anyone really wanted them to. In May of 1920, with the season having just barely begun, the Brooklyn nine participated in the longest game (26 innings; score, 1–1) in the history of the major leagues, a record that still stands. It was this persis-

1 9 5 BROOKLYN DODGERS NATIONAL LEAGUE CHAMPIONS

PATRON MUST ENTER GATE
UPON PURCHASING TICKET

804

PAVILION

BROOKLYN DODGERS
EBBETS FIELD

NATIONAL of AMERICAN LEAGUE

RAIN CHECK
RETAIN THIS CHECK

GAME 3

EBBETS FIELD
BROOKLYN DODGERS
19-17

PAVILION
$1.00

GAMES
3

tence, no doubt, that helped win them the National League pennant later in the year. During that 1920 World Series, Brooklyn suffered an embarrassment at the hands of an American League team that wasn't easily forgotten. Cleveland's second baseman, with the unlikely name of Bill Wambsganss, pulled off an *unassisted* triple play against the Dodgers, the first ever recorded in a World Series game. With heads-up ball like that, it wasn't much of a surprise that Brooklyn wound up losing the Series. And for the next twenty-one excruciatingly long years, the Dodgers continued to add to that depressing record, winning not one pennant in all that time.

It was near the end of those two fallow decades that Larry (Leland Stanford) MacPhail joined the club as its president, bringing with him showmanship, drive, the capacity to build pride, and connections in the Brooklyn Trust Company. He arrived only a few weeks after Leo "the Lip" Durocher joined to manage the team; both benefitted from the combination. He recruited Red Barber, "the Ol' Redhead," to drawl the Dodger games to the multitudes play-by-play. (Radio had come by then.) MacPhail introduced night baseball to Ebbets Field and, wouldn't you know it, in their first game under the new lights, the Dodgers lost—in a no-hitter, no less. Though not quite what the fans had hoped to see that evening, given the Dodgers' reputation, they weren't totally unprepared.

When the Flock finally won the pennant in 1941, pandemonium did reign in Brooklyn. Celebrations erupted all over the borough, topped by a rambunctious parade through the streets of downtown. Who can forget the ragout of names on the team roster?

The Dodgers posed for the official team photograph every year, but this one shows Brooklyn's only world championship team, the 1955 team that took the Yankees in that year's World Series.

There was Dixie Walker, referred to as "Da People's Cherce." There was "Pistol Pete" Reiser. And Dolf Camilli, Joe Medwick, Pee Wee Reese, Cookie Lavagetto. And don't forget Whitlow Wyatt—a great pitcher—Billy Herman, Kirby Higbe, and Mickey Owen. But did the Dodgers win that World Series? Alas, no! So what else is new?

To increase even further the fans' fanaticism and their devotion to the Dodgers' cause, MacPhail brought in organist Gladys Goodding to spice up the scene. On one of her first performances she impetuously played *Three Blind Mice* as three umpires ventured forth onto the playing field, thus ensuring her immortality—among Dodger fans at least, if not among umpires. Other nitwit antics were encouraged: Hilda Chester, heeding her doctor's advice to exercise her arm in the sun, became a regular in the Ebbets Field bleachers by swinging a four-pound cowbell. "The Dodger Sym-Phony," a five-piece band wearing tattered clothes and playing battered instruments, regularly rendered cacophonous support for the home team while mocking the visitors.

The bandbox stadium that was Ebbets Field, shoehorned into an odd-sized lot on the far side of Prospect Park by the unre-nowned design firm of C. A. Buskirk, was itself a curiosity. A long fly ball hitting the Abe Stark (men's clothing) sign would mean extra bases for the lucky batter as well as a new suit from Stark's Pitkin Avenue store. Abe later became Borough President. Lo-

cally brewed Schaefer Beer capitalized on the scoreboard's importance to fans by electrifying two letters luckily contained in its name: the H for "hit" and the E for "error." (Filling out a scorecard in Ebbets Field became a subliminal cue for having another beer, brewing then being one of Brooklyn's important industries.)

When all was said and done, the Dodgers were just the mythic icing on Brooklyn's cake. No one who lived in Brooklyn in those years was unaffected. And no one who asked, "Are you really from Brooklyn?" ever got a curt reply.

When the Dodgers did win a pennant, Brooklyn really celebrated. Here, in 1956, Borough Hall is all decked out in bunting when Borough President John Cashmore did double duty as chairman of the reception committee.

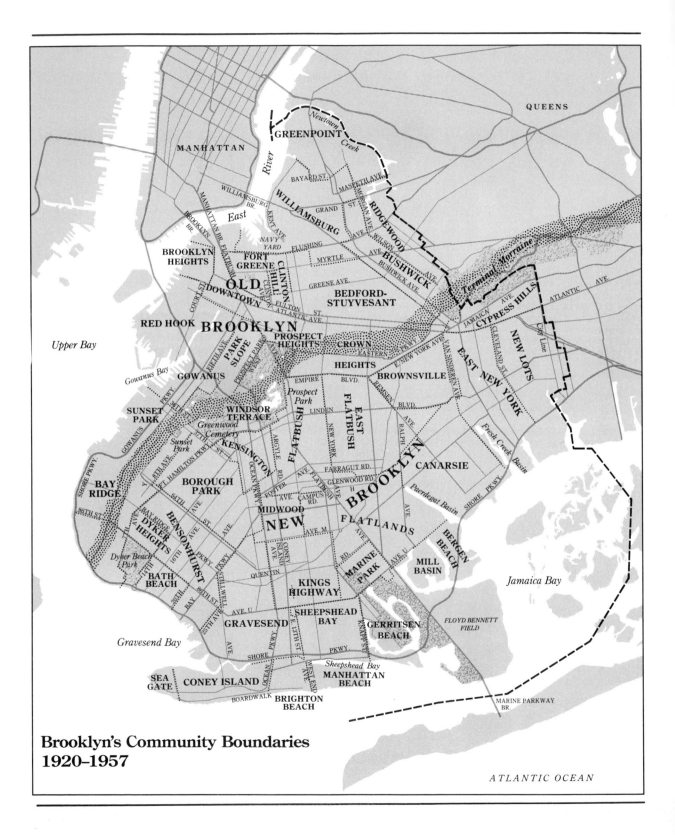

Brooklyn's Community Boundaries
1920–1957

2

WHAT KIND OF PLACE WAS IT?

ad Brooklyn's development resembled that of Queens, where individual neighborhood names have always overshadowed those of county and borough, mail would today be addressed directly to Flatbush, N.Y., instead of Brooklyn, 11226. As it turned out, with the advent of the nineteenth century, the impatient settlers of the Village of Brooklyn—that's all it was—were already beginning to have dreams of establishing a city of their own, like neighboring Manhattan—New York City—across the river. Even though the villagers realized that the Town of Brooklyn that surrounded them had a population just approaching thirty thousand, their political leadership began to pressure the state legislature to reclassify the township. So, in 1834, the Town of Brooklyn officially became a city, the City of Brooklyn—a city on paper, at least. Armed with that label, the area quickly grew in population to exceed even the most optimistic of its promoters' expectations. As a result, the City of Brooklyn expanded its boundaries through the remainder of the century, absorbing one neighboring town after another, until 1896, when the City of Brooklyn's boundaries came to correspond to those of the County of Kings. Yet, as Brooklyn's ambitions were being achieved, adjacent New York City's were growing at an even greater rate—three years later the City of Brooklyn itself was absorbed by the larger entity, becoming one of the five boroughs of Greater New York City. That was on January 1, 1898.

Coming from any of the places that today comprise Brooklyn's neighborhoods doesn't guarantee an awareness of its history. With

Neighborhood designations and boundaries fluctuate and are open to varied opinions; those indicated on the map include only the ones commonly accepted during the period.

The towns and villages of Kings County.

Brooklyn's ancient town lines as invisible as the equator (except for the one set in brass into the Botanic Garden's pavement), what landmarks were there that clearly sang of the borough's heritage? Old houses were simply places where "other people" lived, or maybe—appearing abandoned—were dubbed "haunted." Newer houses offered even less reason to be curious, they were so abundant—and so bland. It was common for kids to call the paths through empty lots and shorefront marshes "Indian trails," but no one ever really attempted to check whether they actually were. Nor did anyone pay much attention to the factories or warehouses or gas tanks, except to complain about their noise or smell or ugliness. Trolley lines were for putting pennies on the tracks of, or hitching a ride on, and not too often for tracing their routes, either through space or time. The educational establishment didn't

FAIRCHILD AERIAL SURVEYS INC. N.Y.C.

help much. As far as school was concerned, history was what took place long ago and preferably far away, not anything that might have been made by people like you or me or anyone we knew or were descended from. History was memory, memorizing names and dates, battles and places, kings and queens—but not the boroughs, thank you. Connections between how things got to be the way we knew them were rarely investigated, except by those rare teachers whose names you can still remember. Victims of McCarthy-era witch hunts, some of them.

So what about those places we came from, or where our cousins did, or the kids we met at the beach or at the pool or in camp? How did those neighborhoods come to be in the first place, and how did they fit into the geography and history of Brooklyn? Is it too late for a bit of history?

Between 1636, when the first Europeans claimed lands that are now Brooklyn's, until the 1920s, when, as we've noted, Kings

The wetlands along Jamaica Bay, still far from developed in this 1934 photograph, resembled what Brooklyn's Dutch must have seen when they first explored the outer reaches of their seventeenth-century settlement.

The Long Island Historical Society building looks pretty much the same today with its new name, the Brooklyn Historical Society, but one-way traffic on Pierrepont Street went in the opposite direction in the late thirties.

County's residential construction boom set a record for the entire nation, a great many place names evolved, some of them remaining to label the neighborhoods that today make up Brooklyn, some reflecting the origins of the European settlers themselves. Not unpredictably, the earliest Dutch chose the Old World name of Breukelen, familiar to them as a village a few miles outside of Amsterdam, to identify their New World settlement, which coincidentally lay only a few miles outside of *New* Amsterdam. In a similar fashion, Midwout in the Netherlands' north became Midwood in Brooklyn's middle, and Gravesend derived from its English founder's hometown on the River Thames, just across London's current eastern boundary. Others, like Gowanus or Canarsie, were adapted from the place names coined by the Native American settlers who preceded the Dutch, the Canarsie Indians (spelled Canar*see,* according to some pedants—in wampum alphabet, no doubt). Other names emerged from the imagination of real-estate developers: Bensonhurst-by-the-Sea was founded as a seaside community on the Benson family lands. Similarly, enclaves of what was then suburban housing were built and baptized Parkville, Ditmas Park, Mapleton Park, or Prospect Park South. Others took on the names Blythebourne, Kings Lawn, Beverly Square West, South Greenfield, Fiske Terrace, or the pun, Tennis Court,

In 1924 the Brooklyn City Railroad Company purchased a hundred bulbous, drop center, maroon-and-cream-colored trolley cars known to railroad buffs as Peter Witt cars, originally developed in the Cleveland streetcar system. Eventually they populated all of Brooklyn.

to mention only a few. The telephone company helped in the process. It reinforced the names of some neighborhoods by labeling exchanges after them: Williamsburg, Greenpoint, Bushwick, Bedford, Flatbush, Hamilton. Other exchanges remind us of local streets—Nevins, Stagg, Henry, Decatur, even Shore Road—and yet others were named after more generalized areas: South, Prospect, and Main in downtown Brooklyn. When the phone company ran out of place names, it named exchanges after flowers: Forsythia never made it; Hyacinth did!

After the Dutch ended their brief stay, the methodical British linked into one county, called Kings, the six townships the Dutch had recognized: Bushwick, Flatbush, Flatlands, New Utrecht, Gravesend, and of course the Town of Brooklyn itself, which encompassed today's downtown and the lands to the east and south. Much later, another town was created by lopping off what had been eastern Flatbush. Labeled New Lots, its name seemed to tell its story: a tract of largely vacant land yearning for development. Most of the town names define neighborhoods to this day—but ones that don't quite correspond to the original boundaries. New Utrecht has fallen out of favor as a place name (except, of course, to those attending that high school). And those who live in historic but somber-sounding Gravesend tend to find other names for where they live.

Brooklyn politicians have had a penchant for redressing the shortcomings of the past, as far as place names are concerned. Gravesend Avenue proved so unpopular that it was recast in the early 1930s as McDonald Avenue. The new name was that of John R. McDonald, then recently chief clerk of the Kings County Surrogate's Court. His advice in divvying up the surrogate's bounty among local widows, orphans, and court-appointed trustees (linked to the political needs of the county Democratic Committee) must have been sufficiently valuable for his name to be memorialized bituminously. For those who wonder how so venerable a name in Brooklyn history as Gravesend, dating back to the 1600s, could be replaced by that of a court clerk—even chief clerk of the Surrogate's Court—consider also that the Civic Center's Washington Street, named for President George, recently met with an equally gravesend fate, carrying today the frolicsome title Cadman Plaza East, in response to a poetic need (whose?) to echo its sister street across the narrow park called Cadman Plaza. As "C.P. East" erased the name Washington, "C.P. West" wiped out the name of lower Fulton Street, which honored Robert Fulton, whose

Bird's-Eye Map of Brooklyn, Showing Location of our THREE DEVELOPED TRACTS Oak Crest, The Lindens, Kings Oaks, (indicated by solid red), and of our as yet undeveloped and un-named properties (red cross-bars).

It will be seen that all our holdings are or will be on the line of the Best Transportation Facilities and IN THE VERY Heart of Brooklyn.

1814 steam ferry was decisive in the early urbanization of that part of Brooklyn. So goes urban history.

Like the history of any old community, Brooklyn's is one of settlement, development, resettlement, and change. And those successive events leave evidence of themselves not only in musty archives but on the very face of the community.

The process of vital change and growth continues, sometimes with punctuations of dormancy and decay. Between 1920 and 1957, Brooklyn's empty spaces were largely wiped out. Since then, abandonment and demolition have created new spaces and new developments. These, as well as the rediscoveries of old resources temporarily out of fashion—and therefore overlooked or forgotten—will yet again change the face of Brooklyn.

Real estate advertising of the twenties stressed that the heart of Brooklyn lay in the outlying communities being opened up for development along the routes of the expanding subway lines.

3

HOW DID IT GET THAT WAY?

rooklyn is really *two* Brooklyns. "Old" Brooklyn had already been built by the time of World War I. The other, much larger "new" Brooklyn began to be intensively built up by developers—let's call them speculators—following the Armistice. The process wasn't really "finished" until after World War II. And with the development of the new Brooklyn came the inevitable change in the old.

Generally speaking, old Brooklyn was the part closest to Manhattan. It corresponded to the old Kings County towns of Brooklyn and Bushwick. It stretched from Brooklyn Heights, Cobble Hill, Red Hook, and Sunset Park on the west to the farthest edge of Bedford-Stuyvesant and Williamsburg on the east; from Greenpoint on the north to Park Slope, Windsor Terrace, and lower Crown Heights on the south.

Everything old in Brooklyn doesn't lie north of Eastern Parkway's glacial ridge—nor does everything new lie south of it. Some of Brooklyn's oldest relics, like its wonderful Dutch and English colonial farmhouses, have miraculously survived amid the rows of houses in Flatbush, Flatlands, New Utrecht, and East New York. But the greatest concentration of old Brooklyn, block after block of it, survives up north, from Newtown Creek down to the area around Greenwood Cemetery, from the East River and Upper Bay out to City Line.

What was old Brooklyn like between the wars, and how did it change during and just after that period?

Take Brooklyn Heights, for example, the charming residential quarter between Borough Hall and the piers along the harbor. In

Just before opening in the early forties, Gowanus Parkway seemed like a toy—just four lanes limited to autos only—compared to today's expressway that envelops a widened Third Avenue in threatening shadow. Even then, enough traffic was expected to use the parkway to warrant Bush Terminal's painting the gargantuan billboard advertising its real estate.

the early nineteenth century it was one of Manhattan's first suburbs, removed from the bustle of the nascent city and yet pleas-
antly accessible by ferry. Once industrialization came to Brooklyn,
the community found itself adjoining an industrialized East River
shore, yet it remained above it all—literally so, some eighty feet
above. Down below were the New York Dock Company warehouses, busy wharves and ships, and the Squibb Pharmaceutical
factories. On the far side of the Brooklyn Bridge, the Arbuckle
Brothers stored Yuban Coffee in the Empire Stores. But up top,
along Columbia Heights and other streets demurely hidden from
the remainder of downtown Brooklyn, brownstone row houses
and a few taller turn-of-the-century hotels provided an exclusive
enclave for the mostly well-to-do.

Only a stone's throw away, however, lay a squalid industrial
neighborhood—called "Irishtown" at the end of the nineteenth
century—leading to the Brooklyn Navy Yard. The name Vinegar
Hill, the rise overlooking the Yard, has recently been reintro-
duced, its early-1800s Irish residents having dubbed it so after a
similar place made famous in the 1798 Irish Rebellion. The maids
and handymen of the brownstone Heights came from this area
across the tracks, streetcar tracks set into the street, and others
high in the air—those of the Fulton Street elevated. Until it was
taken down in 1941, the shadows and noise of the old el made it
very clear where the Heights ended and the rest of Brooklyn
began.

Irishtown and environs were a gray place. Nuzzling the Yard
was the Brooklyn Edison Company's Hudson Avenue plant, a
technological marvel to combustion engineers but a nuisance to
residents. Its stacks regularly belched smoke onto the local scene,
one that was already contaminated by the aroma of slaughter-
houses. With Edison and all the other industry close by, no amount
of bleach could whiten the clothes blowing on the clotheslines.
Between the Brooklyn Bridge and Manhattan Bridge approaches,
workers in the concrete structures of the multistory Gair City
made cardboard cartons to package America. The familiar brown
cakes of Kirkman's Laundry Soap were made on Water Street,
and the equally familiar Brillo pads were also produced close by.
Masury and Atlantic and National made paint there, when linseed
oil and white lead were still the crucial ingredients.

Sands Street's ramshackle bars and boardinghouses had their
cheap liquor, and even cheaper women, waiting for the next group
of Navy Yard sailors to arrive from their weeks or months of

enforced chastity on the high seas. Some called the area the Barbary Coast of the East. The slums of Sands Street, Navy Street, and their surroundings, where Brooklynites like "Scarface" Al Capone and Willie "the Actor" Sutton first saw the light of day, finally fell to the wrecker's ball at the end of World War II, replaced by so-called slum-clearance housing. Reformers were marketing the idea that improving the way the poor were housed would by itself improve the potential of their children. The cynical Robert Moses understood other values of slum clearance.

Among the monotony of low-rent housing, the unkempt miscellanies of unused greenspace, and the roar of the Brooklyn-Queens Expressway, just try to find an address on Sands Street today. No more slums.

The significant historical and architectural landmark of old Brooklyn is its 1849 City Hall, called, since 1898, Borough Hall. It evokes the early urban history of the place. Its steep front steps face the street curving up the hill from Fulton Ferry; symbolically, they greet arrivals from Manhattan. The Hall presides over what little is left of the old downtown.

Downtown wasn't a place where many people chose to live, not if they could afford to live elsewhere. But at the turn of the twentieth century and into its first decades, Brooklyn's civic, financial, entertainment, and shopping heart was its traditional downtown, radiating from the intersection of Fulton and Flatbush. Legitimate theaters found their place throughout the area and some remain— unused—to this day along Fulton Street. In the thirties, many a young fellow, playing hooky from high school, was able to catch a matinee striptease at Minsky's (properly BILLY MINSKY BROOKLYN BURLESQUE) on Hudson Avenue where the New York Telephone company stands today. Downtown was easily accessible and, even more important, a desirable place to visit. Crowds were everywhere, and as in any city's downtown, the pace and noise and dust were the price you paid for the convenience.

The decade of the twenties marked an explosion of skyscraper office tower construction along Court Street and vicinity, just as it did in lower and midtown Manhattan. The wedding-cake form of Court Chambers at 66 Court Street joined the height sweepstakes in 1926 at 415 feet. The 16 Court Building topped out at 390 feet. New York Telephone Company's Brooklyn headquarters, the area's most distinguished tower, designed by talented Art-Deco architect Ralph Walker, lifted itself 348 feet above Willoughby Street. And in 1929 Brooklyn's tallest building, the Williamsburgh

Brooklyn Heights's brownstones and hotels preside over the bustling 1930s waterfront. Furman Street, on the right, passes under Montague Street's slope, then a connection to the East River shore.

Savings Bank's 512-foot tower, opened its doors. These, together with the St. George Hotel tower (315 feet) and the pinnacles of the Towers Hotel practically next door, began to give downtown a skyline of consequence. But as the perception of downtown's location was being made more evident, downtown itself was beginning to lose its functional and symbolic importance.

Left over from the Victorian period were the department stores west of Flatbush, and the theaters to the east. To meet the needs of the varied audiences, there were restaurants—or at least places to eat—to suit every pocketbook. Farther west, in the Borough Hall section, were the courts and bail bondsmen and politicos. Farther down Fulton Street, toward the old ferry, were all kinds of shops no longer fashionable by the twenties, and destined to become one of Brooklyn's antique (junk?) rows.

The Brooklyn Academy of Music—today called BAM—had moved to its new building near the Long Island Rail Road's Atlantic Avenue terminal in 1912, bringing a new wave of culture to the area. Among the highlights of the twenties, thirties, and forties were recitals by Sergei Rachmaninoff, Fritz Kreisler, Ignace Paderewski, and America's own Paul Robeson, among many, many luminaries. It was on BAM's stage in December of 1920 that Enrico Caruso collapsed in what proved to be his next-to-last public appearance. The Boston Symphony performed every season without fail under the baton of Pierre Monteux until 1923–24, followed by Serge Koussevitzky, and then Charles Munch. Dance companies of the importance of Anna Pavlova and the Ballet Russe as well as the Denishawn Dancers graced the boards. Travelogues were a must, with Burton Holmes, while Frank Buck

Furman Street's warehouses were still in place as strollers enjoyed a walk along Brooklyn Heights's Promenade, atop the incomplete Brooklyn-Queens Expressway. How peaceful this brief, carless interlude must have been.

periodically spiced the scene with descriptions of how he "brought 'em back alive." Nor were current events neglected on the lecture circuit: Sgt. Alvin York spoke in 1929, Winston Churchill in '31 and '32, architect Frank Lloyd Wright described "My Life and Work" the next year, H. V. Kaltenborn, a Brooklyn boy, discoursed in 1936 on the Spanish Civil War, and there were others, including Sinclair Lewis, Eleanor Roosevelt, Thomas Mann, and Wendell Willkie. After the war, poet Langston Hughes appeared, as did Jawaharlal Nehru, playwright Eugene O'Neill, Ogden Nash, and even Alistair Cooke, long before TV was presenting "Masterpiece Theatre."

On the far side of downtown and very close to BAM lay the Fort Greene neighborhood, named for the adjacent high-rising park and its colossal Doric monument by architect Stanford White to the twelve thousand prisoners who died at the hands of the

Brooklyn's Civic Center looked different in 1941. The egg-shaped dome of the Kings County Courthouse, where Brooklyn Law School stands today, complements Borough Hall's cupola. Henry Ward Beecher's bronze statue surveyed the scene close up. The Fulton Street el still stands even though service ended in 1940.

British during the Revolution. A community built of small-scale row houses, the area began to lose its stability in the period between the wars with the seemingly inevitable conversion to rooming houses.

Just beyond Fort Greene lay the Pratt Institute area, which retained a gentility reminiscent of Brooklyn Heights and a name that also alluded, in the best Marquand manner, to its elevated position: Clinton Hill. Although the children of the Institute's founder, Charles Pratt, moved out of Brooklyn in the twenties, other older and affluent Brooklynites continued to reside for a time in the area's fine mansions along Clinton and Washington avenues and nearby side streets.

Wrapping around the Institute on the north, east, and south was an industrial belt where Mergenthaler and Intertype manufactured 99 percent of the world's typesetting machinery; where Griffin

The twenties' building boom gave Brooklyn its distinctive Court Street skyscrapers. This 1927 view from Brooklyn Heights's Towers Hotel roof also shows the old Mansion House hotel, in the foreground, on Hicks Street before it was taken down in the thirties for namesake apartments.

shoe polish was made; where Pioneer ice cream was produced by a division of the Borden Milk Company. Washington Avenue continued north past the Wallabout Market, Brooklyn's colorful wholesale produce mart. At the start of World War II, the mock-Flemish buildings and stalls were demolished to expand the Navy Yard. At Park Avenue stood the factories—today in sad disrepair—of the Rockwood Chocolate and Cocoa Company, among the world's largest chocolate manufacturers, second in size only to Hershey's.

Southeast of Clinton Hill lay Bedford, a community with eighteenth-century roots, and the adjacent nineteenth-century brownstones of Stuyvesant Heights, some half-dozen blocks farther east. Few who knew the area made the connection that its north-south avenues had been named for the state's governors: Marcy, Tompkins, Throop, Lewis, and Stuyvesant, the last for old peg-legged Peter himself. On the other hand, few forgot its

Downtown used to be dead on Sundays before shopping became a seven-day-a-week thing. The empty streets made it a natural for architectural photography like Abraham & Straus's new Art Deco east building annex at Livingston and Hoyt streets, opened late in 1929. Earlier that year A & S, Bloomingdale's, and Filenes formed with other stores the Federated Department Store Group.

hyphenated appellation, Bedford-Stuyvesant, a name coined in an early 1930s survey by the Brooklyn Edison Company.

Until the end of World War II the Bed-Stuy area embraced a mixture of religions reflected in the spires, campaniles, and domes projecting prominently above its brownstone-scaled skyline. At Bedford and Lafayette avenues was Temple Israel, whose exotic Near Eastern forms were to be bowdlerized when its Reform Jewish membership moved away and it came to be used as a municipal traffic court, and later a linoleum discount store.

Bed-Stuy's southern edge was demarked by two modes of rapid transit only two blocks apart, the unsightly old Fulton Street elevated and the Long Island Rail Road's equally unkempt Atlantic Avenue route. In this, the least desirable part of the neighborhood, a black community began to grow in the twenties, its residents attracted by lower rents and, more important, the willingness of landlords to rent to them. A black ghetto formed, which steadily expanded northward, until one day it would surpass Harlem in black population. Reformers soon began to agitate for the removal of the noisome elevated (some, no doubt, privately

Pratt Institute's campus looked more like Prospect Park in 1925 when the mothers of Clinton Hill converged there to sun their infants in elaborate baby carriages.

Central Congregational Church, on Hancock Street in Bed-Stuy, was a sanctuary clad in corrugated iron. In the forties, when this picture was taken, it was occupied by the Holy Trinity Baptist Church. In 1948 it was demolished to build P.S. 3.

hoping for the removal of the blacks as well). By the late twenties the city itself decided to enter the rapid-transit business and started construction of the first IND route (under Fulton Street), which would make the old el redundant. When opened in 1933, the route linked Bed-Stuy with Harlem and, in 1941, after most of the el had been demolished, inspired the Duke Ellington–Billy Strayhorn number, "Take the A Train."

The edges of Bed-Stuy filled with small industries. One of the most interesting was the American Merri-Lei Corporation, founded in 1927 at 918 Halsey Street, across from the trolley barn. It had the distinction of being the world's largest producer of Hawaiian leis, larger even than any Hawaiian manufacturer. As a matter of fact, Hawaii was Merri-Lei's best customer, selling its products in Honolulu for fifteen cents each, while in Brooklyn's five-and-tens they were only a dime.

Bedford Avenue, from Fulton Street up the hill to Eastern Parkway, became Brooklyn's original automobile row, and many of the showroom structures remain, such as Studebaker at the northeast corner of Sterling Place. The New Muse, the neighborhood museum at Lincoln Place, has found a use for one of those show-rooms, which itself reused the former site of the Bedford Restaurant, popular in the early years of the twentieth century. Farther east along Fulton Street, in Bed-Stuy's center, was the Sheffield Milk Company. Today its dairy and bottling plant, adaptively reworked, form parts of Bedford-Stuyvesant Restoration Corporation's Restoration Plaza.

To the south of these communities, but still lying within the boundaries of the old Town of Brooklyn, lay a widely differing group of neighborhoods that stretched all the way from the shores of Upper New York Bay to what in the twenties came to be called Broadway Junction, after the complicated subway station on steel stilts where Bed-Stuy, Williamsburg, and East New York petered out and subway yards, trolley barns, and cemeteries converged.

At the western end, the harbor end, of this string of precincts was a catchall area called South Brooklyn. It included the tall gray concrete structures and adjacent piers of Bush Terminal, built just before the start of World War I, and the unseemly grain elevators on the Henry Street Basin, built by the Port Authority after the conflict ended. Virginia Dare extracts are still processed on Third Avenue; Topps Chewing Gum was once manufactured in a Bush Terminal loft, as were (beginning in 1951) the renowned Topps Baseball Cards.

Traffic along Bedford Avenue, the borough's automobile row in the early days of the car, became so heavy in the 1920s that the Police Department had to install a traffic tower at Grant Square, just like those along Fifth Avenue in Manhattan.

The Culver Line el, part of its route running along Fifth Avenue and part on Third, helped settle the area inland from the piers of Upper Bay. Diminutive two- and three-story row houses pranced up the slopes of a neighborhood that came to be called Sunset Park after the six-block green space of that name.

The term today describes a larger area, stretching all the way to the malls of Leif Erikson Square at 66th Street. This area became, in the early twentieth century, the home of many Scandinavians, drawn there by its nearness to the port of Brooklyn and the seafaring and shipbuilding jobs it spawned. A mark of their settlement is the array of institutions they founded—Norwegian Hospital, Lutheran Hospital, and Imatra, the Finnish social and benevolent society still to be found on 40th Street, to name just a few.

Also included in South Brooklyn by general agreement were the tough neighborhoods of Red Hook and Gowanus, which contained the gas tanks, industrial facilities, wharves, and shipbuilding yards along Gowanus Bay, Buttermilk Channel, and the famed but not-so-sweet-smelling Gowanus Canal. (When the vats of one paint factory along the Gowanus were cleaned, the dark green canal bloomed with scarlet and gold and issued blue infernal bubbles.) Red Hook and its neighbor, Gowanus, were gritty working-class areas where you were trained early for the hard knocks of making it in Brooklyn, whether by the straight road or another. Red Hook was where Al Capone hung out when his family moved from near downtown to 38 Garfield Place, and it was on Red Hook's streets that he acquired the wound that gave him his nickname "Scarface." It was also a place for tanneries. Ever smell a tannery? The Gowanus masked the aroma.

In the heyday of the twenties, the yachts of the wealthy were repaired in the Tebo Yacht Basin. In the early thirties the shanties of a Depression-caused Hooverville arose close-by. With the coming of the New Deal, the squatters were evicted and the area converted by WPA workers into the much admired Red Hook Play Center. During World War II the Todd Shipyards, the largest boat-repair yard in the country, built landing craft for the expected Allied invasion needs, and in 1946 the burned-out hulk of the once-great French ocean liner, the *Normandie* (officially renamed the USS *Lafayette* when recommissioned as a troopship) was towed there in preparation for its final scrapping.

In the fifties, as Brooklyn Heights once again began to attract interest as an in-town middle-class community, some newcomers

spilled south over Atlantic Avenue, suggesting a need to rename the northern parts of what people there still called Red Hook. Cobble Hill and Carroll Gardens, dreamed up by the real-estate fraternity, were charming choices in their own way. Thomas Wolfe had discovered a basement apartment at 40 Verandah Place in 1931 and described it in *You Can't Go Home Again*: "The place may seem to you more like a dungeon than a room that a man would voluntarily elect to live in. It is long and narrow . . . and the only natural light that enters it comes from two small windows rather high up in the wall, facing each other at the opposite ends, and these are heavily guarded with iron bars to keep the South Brooklyn thugs from breaking in."

To the east of the lands that drained into the creek that was later tidied up to become the Gowanus Canal were the brownstoned streets of Park Slope. At the low end was light manufacturing, like the Higgins Ink Company on Eighth Street, makers of India and other inks. At the crest, in the nineteenth century, lived the canal's developer, transcontinental railroad magnate Edwin C.

J. P. Morgan's yacht, the *Corsair*, in the foreground, as well as the *Flying Fox*, the *United States*, and the *Genessee*, are among those bundled up for winter storage in the Tebo Yacht Basin in Red Hook in 1928.

Looking like some Jonathan Swift war machine, the Gowanus Parkway viaduct rises precipitously to clear the Canal's demanding height restrictions established by the War Department in the uncertain days preceding World War II.

Litchfield, in the mansion in Prospect Park that has since served as the Park Department's Brooklyn headquarters. Development of the easternmost blocks—the "park blocks"—which were the highest in elevation and the most desirable, was interrupted periodically by financial panics. In Brooklyn, as elsewhere, the more affluent were not only higher in the social scale but also higher on the land. As desirable as the park blocks were, the most desirable of all were the northernmost ones, called the Gold Coast, fronting the park closest to Grand Army Plaza, the great Civil War memorial that had been built in 1870 in the style of Paris. The Tilyou family, owners of Coney Island's Steeplechase Park, lived in an old mansion they had bought in 1912 at the corner of Garfield Place, until rising land values in 1928 caused them to sell. The stately fifteen-story apartment at 35 Prospect Park West was built on the site, and the Tilyous moved back, to a large top-floor apartment from which, on a clear day, they could see the ocean and the lights of Coney Island.

In the twenties the Gold Coast spilled over to nearby Eastern Parkway, where the greenway began its trek eastward from Grand Army Plaza. The parkway was a creation of Olmsted and Vaux, like Prospect Park and Grand Army Plaza.

The phalanx of fireproof, high-rise apartment structures across from so-called Institute Park emphasized the crest of the glacial ridge along the parkway to those who lived in adjacent low-rise Prospect Heights, which lay along the incline that rose southward from Atlantic Avenue. With names like Copley Plaza at number 41

SERIOUSLY INJURED
ON BROOKLYN STREETS THIS YEAR
0 6 5
SLOW UP
FATAL ACCIDENTS THIS YEAR   FATAL ACCIDENTS THIS WEEK
0 0 2   0 2
WHAT'S YOUR HURRY?
MAKE
BROOKLYN SAFE
BROOKLYN
SAFETY COUNCIL

("The Aristocrat of Apartment Buildings"), Turner Towers—originally named the Park Avenue Apartments—at 135, and Adelphi Hall at 201 ("Every Room an Outside Room"), these were very prestigious places to live. Professional offices on the lower floors made the strip one of Brooklyn's most desirable doctors rows.

On Eastern Parkway's south side stood McKim, Mead & White's Brooklyn Museum, whose monumental entrance steps were demolished in the mid-thirties. Inside was one of the world's finest collections of Egyptian art, with mummies to captivate even the most sullen of young visitors. Next door was the plain parkway entrance to the Brooklyn Botanic Garden, finally embellished in 1946 by a gift from Michael and Bessie Tuch, who lived at number 135 across from the site. Closest to the Plaza were the weather-beaten ruins of the long-interrupted Brooklyn Public Library project. When the redesigned main library building finally opened there in 1941, *The New Yorker* critic Lewis Mumford wrote with elation, "Put alongside the Widener Library at Harvard, the Yale Library, the Harkness [*sic*] at Columbia, the Congressional, or the New York Public Library, Brooklyn's new one is tops."

Completing the itinerary of neighborhoods that formed the old Town of Brooklyn was Crown Heights, earlier named Crow Hill

As the number of cars traversing Brooklyn's main thoroughfares multiplied, safety signs like this one at Grand Army Plaza were installed to caution against speeding. Police officers' hats in the 1920s looked more like those of fire fighters.

or Crow Heights, nasty designations for the area's early black settlement. Crown Heights lay to the east of Prospect Heights and Institute Park, straddling both the north and south sides of Eastern Parkway. During the Depression and into the forties, a "slave market" developed near the Bedford Avenue intersection, where those who could afford household help would drive by to choose among black women who congregated there looking for jobs. The going rate was twenty to thirty-five cents an hour.

Crown Heights saw a redevelopment in the 1920s with the construction of fine walkup and elevator apartments that builders began to slip into the ranks of its picturesque, early-twentieth-century row housing and on sites formerly occupied by Victorian mansions. Along tree-lined streets appeared stately elevator apartments with pseudo-Tudor half-timbered façades and Tudor-sounding names. Buckingham Hall Apartments, on St. Mark's Avenue, was touted in the ads as "beyond comparison, located as it is, on the most exclusive avenue in Brooklyn." It offered prospective tenants an inner garden court, plug-in outlets for radios, an open-air roof garden and playground, and Murphy-In-A-Door beds in the smaller units. There were even a formal dining room and ballroom for its residents' exclusive use.

As part of the movement to bring social as well as religious cohesion to middle-class Jewish life, the city was seeing construction of Jewish Centers, such as the one at 667 Eastern Parkway,

In 1916, young city farmers were busy in the Brooklyn Botanic's Children's Garden. Silhouetted behind them was the picturesque complex of breweries that would soon feel the impact of Prohibition.

in the heart of Crown Heights, which was cloaked with a blandly ostentatious neo-Classical façade. (In this as in other such centers sprinkled across Brooklyn, it was an institution called the *shvitz*, the Russian-style steambath, that provided a strong cohesive force among the community's men, stronger sometimes than that of religion. The J.C.'s *shvitz* became the upwardly mobile substitute for the ones they left on the Lower East Side or at Coney Island—their sauna, in other words.) Operatic star Richard Tucker began his singing career in this building as a cantor. The Brooklyn Jewish Center today is a yeshiva of the Lubovitcher movement of Chasidim, a group that moved into the area after World War II and whose world headquarters is on the other side of the parkway, at number 770.

North of what was once the Town of Brooklyn—and still within "old" Brooklyn—lay today's communities of Williamsburg, Greenpoint, and Bushwick-Ridgewood, once making up the former Town of Bushwick.

Williamsburg had long been settled when, in 1903, the bridge bearing the same name connected it with Manhattan's teeming Delancey Street. Williamsburg had been briefly a city in its own right. When it was absorbed by the expanding City of Brooklyn in 1855 it acquired the title "Eastern District," to distinguish it from its new parent, the "Western District," which ran westward to downtown.

Those newcomers who could afford them moved into so-called "New Law" walkup apartments that were built just for them, and the others, the preponderant number, moved into the older, humbler, more vernacular accommodations. These were adapted from older wood-frame row houses clad in decorative wooden shingles. These "tenements" would later become notorious as firetraps when maintenance first became more uneconomical, and then more sporadic. They were labeled slums, and the nation's first New Deal, Depression-inspired slum-clearance project—for years America's largest—the modernistic Williamsburg Houses, replaced many of them. Nearby Grand Street attracted a mix of neighborhood-oriented stores whose products and smells, as well as the languages of their proprietors and customers, conjured up the zestiness of an Old World bazaar.

By the 1920s, Williamsburg's population had stabilized into quite a mix of Eastern European Jews, Italians from the provinces near Naples and from Sicily, and many Ukrainians and Poles. Their

As Brooklyn's population began to move out of "Old" Brooklyn, Eastern Parkway across from the Brooklyn Museum began to resemble nearby Prospect Park West. No. 41 at Underhill Avenue borrowed an aristocratic name from Boston.

Where Broadway sliced diagonally through Brooklyn's street grid, many odd-shaped sites emerged ideally suited to trapezoidal plans of theaters. This one, at the sharp intersection with Howard Avenue, made a perfect spot for a vaudeville palace.

children attended Eastern District High School or one of the nearby Roman Catholic parochial schools. Many of the men worked in the array of industries in the blocks near the East River. Among the largest were those closest to the waterway, such as the Domino Sugar refineries, which are still there. Down Kent Avenue was the F. & M. Schaefer Brewery, established in 1916, just four years before the onset of Prohibition. Schaefer survived to celebrate Repeal with the elevating motto, "Our hand has never lost its skill." Nearby, on Wythe Avenue, I. Rokeach & Sons established a modern factory in 1929 to produce kosher foods. At the other end of Williamsburg, near its border with Queens, Kirsch Beverages began bottling soda in 1927; in the thirties, Kirsch plastered Brooklyn's billboards with ads hawking eight ounces for a nickel.

Silhouetted across the flat green fields of McCarren Park were the verdigris onion domes that identified the Russian Orthodox Cathedral of the Transfiguration, a local landmark since 1921. Beyond lay the community of Greenpoint and its colorful political leader and promoter, Peter J. McGuinness. At various times an alderman, Kings County sheriff and register, and Assistant Commissioner of Brooklyn Borough Works, he was for a long time the undisputed Democratic boss of Greenpoint. It was he who, in 1947, first referred to his beloved community as "Greenpernt, the garden spot of the univoise," a title that has since stuck. He had fought hard to keep the traditions of the neighborhood, like the Greenpoint Ferry, whose final trip in 1933 he personally bemoaned. And he succeeded in getting a bridge constructed alongside Meeker Avenue to link Greenpoint with Queens across Newtown Creek. It was named the Kosciusko, which his Polish constituency sincerely appreciated.

Greenpoint's people, primarily a combination of Irish, Italian, and Polish, also found jobs in the industries that lined the East River and Newtown Creek. Wealthy industrialist Charles Pratt's Standard Oil refineries, producers of the Astral Oil that kept the nineteenth century's kerosene lamps burning, occupied part of this stretch; the refineries themselves were consumed in a spectacular blaze in December of 1930. In 1954, another spectacular, the colossal Iwo Jima flag-raising sculpture was cast in a hundred tons of bronze at the postage-stamp-sized Bedi-Rassy Foundry at 227 India Street. It was the largest structure ever cast in bronze. The statue stands today at the edge of Arlington National Cemetery, overlooking the Potomac. Some say that the success of Eberhard

Faber's yellow Mongol pencils, for decades manufactured on West Street near Kent, was due to the pencil eraser reputed to have been conceived there.

East of Williamsburg and north of Broadway lay Bushwick, a section that stretched all the way to the Queens boundary. (The zigzag border was determined in the early 1920s, thus averting a bloody border dispute between boroughs—ever since the street grid was put in, the border with Queens had run irregularly through people's bedrooms.) In those parts of Bushwick, the neighborhood unpredictably assumed the name Ridgewood, whose texture and population then just crossed the invisible line into Queens, making it difficult for some residents to decide which borough they owed allegiance to. In the early 1900s, some Ridgewood institutions were identifying themselves as being in Brooklyn in order to assume the more desirable cachet.

From the late nineteenth century, the heavily German district of Bushwick had been acclaimed for its dozens of breweries, bearing such delicious names as Obermeyer & Liebman's, Vicelius & Ulmer's Continental Lagerbier Brewery, Leonard Eppig's, and

The small-town atmosphere of a typical American Main Street was as apparent along Greenpoint's Manhattan Avenue in the late twenties as it is today. The trolleys, telephone poles, and "cobblestone" paving are gone, but the spire of St. Anthony's survives.

Neon signs were yet to revolutionize outdoor advertising in America. In the twenties, theaters such as the Greenpoint relied on thousands of flickering light bulbs to call attention to themselves, their silent films, and vaudeville attractions.

John Trommer's. With the coming of Prohibition and the shift of these breweries to the production of sodas and "near-beer," the German families whose men worked the vats began to shift toward the beckoning greenery of Queens, across the line, thus opening the door for a new—Italian—population. St. Barbara's Roman Catholic Church, built at Central Avenue and Bleecker Street with funds from a local German brewer, found itself in the 1940s surrounded by Italian caffès, whose sweet offerings in their own way praised the gleaming white-glazed terra-cotta confection of the church.

Bushwick's posh street was, appropriately, Bushwick Avenue. It had no trolley or rattling elevated lines of its own, even though, over much of its length, it paralleled noisy, gloomy Broadway, just a block away. Still in evidence near Myrtle Avenue are the homes of some beer barons and that of Dr. Frederick Cook, who vied—unsuccessfully, and with more than a little notoriety—with pompous, well-connected Adm. Robert E. Peary for recognition as the first person to reach the North Pole. At the far end of the avenue, near the Cemetery of the Evergreens, was the Trommer Brewery, which not only brewed White Label, a metropolitan favorite, but operated an Old World beer garden and restaurant that was a very popular place indeed. The establishment disappeared with the onset of World War II, the beer itself with the beer strike of 1949.

Bushwick Avenue was also a place where the mayor lived. Between 1918 and 1925, while he was the city's chief magistrate, Mayor John F. Hylan lived in a modest brownstone at number 959, still standing just off Bleecker; Gracie Mansion had not yet been

The Trommer folks not only made beer in their brewery on Bushwick Avenue, near the Cemetery of the Evergreens, but they served it, too, in the popular restaurant they maintained on the site.

TROMMER'S BREWERY RESTAURANT — BROOKLYN, N. Y.

secured as the mayor's official residence, and Manhattan had not yet been chosen as the place where *all* mayors would reside.

These were the neighborhoods of "old" Brooklyn, the Brooklyn that had been almost totally settled and developed by the end of the First World War. With the start of the twenties, a "new" Brooklyn emerged; although it wasn't a Brooklyn of haut-bourgeois architecture, it was the Brooklyn in which many spent significant parts of their lives.

The enormous Iwo Jima statue in Washington, the largest bronze statue in the world, was cast (in sections) at the Bedi-Rassy Art Foundry at 227 India Street, in Greenpoint.

4

IT WAS CERTAINLY CHANGING

he year was 1920. The "war to end all wars" was over; Prohibition and what was to become known as the Roaring Twenties—the Jazz Age—had begun. The scene had been set for the rapid residential development of the flatlands of Brooklyn, southward, all the way to the sea.

The twenties took the nation by storm. The 1920 Census was the first to indicate that America's urban population outnumbered the rural. The year was significant for the borough, as well, heralding, in a sense, the start of a "new" Brooklyn. To many, however, Brooklyn's significant moment had already been its 1898 absorption into Greater New York, which, many feared, signaled the loss of a special identity and character that was widely recognized and regarded.

The twenties were a period when many adjustments were being made in the use of Brooklyn's land. Truck farms and small orchards had largely disappeared. Vacant land grew scarcer. Houses and apartment buildings, as well as small corner store complexes, were going up all over, some replacing earlier structures or filling in the vacant lots between others. Detours were common as sewer and paving projects multiplied. In some areas, private development was so rapid that the streets remained unpaved, and with no sewers to dispose of rainwater, flooding would occur after every downpour.

Many of the sewer and street projects that were left undone in the twenties were undertaken in the next decade by Roosevelt's New Deal, through the Works Projects Administration, the WPA.

The construction of the Williamsburgh Savings Bank Tower overlooking Times Plaza extended Brooklyn's downtown well into Brooklyn's heart, but its completion in 1929 coincided with the stock market crash and an end to the 1920s building boom.

But the thirties had also brought other kinds of projects to the borough—what might be called vernacular architecture—squatters' camps, impromptu settlements peopled by the unemployed. They were called "Hoovervilles," after the defeated Republican president. (With jobs largely nonexistent, a considerable number of the squatters would have given their right arms just to become one of those guys "leaning on their shovels"—as testy Republicans liked to describe WPA workers.)

Many of those who were growing up in the years that followed 1920 were either pioneers settling Brooklyn's newly developing outer fringes or were among some other wave *re*settling the neighborhoods of "old" Brooklyn. With just enough extra housing units as there were takers, it was not uncommon for Brooklyn tenants to play "musical chairs" as the city's traditional yearly moving day—October first—rolled around. Many families experienced both situations, trying both resettlement and new accommodations in the "new" Brooklyn, at least until the housing shortage set in with the start of World War II.

Some just left. The twenties saw the children of Charles Pratt split for other parts, leaving the family's splendid mansions in Clinton Hill for the elegance of Park Avenue and the serenity of Long Island's North Shore. Pratt's son Harold left a mansion at Clinton and Willoughby avenues that was quickly snapped up in 1920 by movie mogul J. Stuart Blackton of Brooklyn's Vitagraph film studios, in Flatbush. (He just as quickly sold it, as moviemaking gravitated from Avenue M to Los Angeles, leaving the limestone-and-brick structure an unsightly ruin for two decades.) Despite such desertions, however, Brooklyn was on the move.

In 1900 the borough numbered 1,166,582 people; by 1950 its population had more than doubled—to 2,738,175. The largest spurt was in the twenties, when a net gain was achieved of more than half a million. Some of these moved into the new apartment houses that were springing up in "old" Brooklyn, ones that increased the density of such earlier, low-rise neighborhoods as those bordering Prospect Park—Flatbush, Park Slope, Crown Heights—as well as Brownsville and sections of Brooklyn Heights, Clinton Hill, and Williamsburg. By the end of the boom and the onset of the Depression, at least one critic complained of the solid rows of apartment buildings on streets like Ocean Avenue, calling it the "Harlemizing" of Brooklyn. He wasn't referring to our image of Harlem as a black ghetto; it was a reference to an earlier period, when Harlem's broad avenues were first being

The twenties brought greater mobility to expanding Brooklyn via dependable motorized trucks: to deliver building materials to new homes under construction, to help families move into those new homes, and to bring them Christmas trees in the proper season.

The Depression was not felt
equally. In 1932, Ocean Avenue's
six-story apartments, like the
Montauk at Woodruff Avenue,
sported striped awnings in many
windows and a classy touring car
parked at the canopy.

developed with its solid rows of apartment buildings, and the
neighborhood was heavily Jewish. Brooklyn didn't lack for open
anti-Semitism.

The vast majority of the borough's newcomers, however,
moved into housing built in Brooklyn's southern tier, on its sandy
outwash plain, left when the ocean retreated from the 40,000-
year-old glacial ridge that sweeps diagonally from Highland Park
to the Narrows across Brooklyn's geography. That area, occupying more than half of Brooklyn's landmass, lies on the ocean side
of the rise that runs through Eastern Parkway, Prospect Park,
Windsor Terrace, and Greenwood Cemetery. It includes the old
Kings County towns of New Utrecht, Gravesend, Flatlands, Flatbush, and New Lots.

For the most part, this flat expanse was the fodder for real-
estate development following the end of World War I. In it, Prospect Park had already been opened and had become an attraction
well before the turn of the century. Builders had created a number
of bucolic Flatbush suburbs along the routes of the steam railroads
to the shore resort of Coney Island. Coney was a seaside "sin
city" long before the nineteenth century's end—by the 1890s,
three racetracks were in full operation nearby. Picturesque harbor
views, interrupted only by the defenses of Fort Hamilton at the
Narrows, made the high ground of Bay Ridge very desirable for
villas and estates. Along Gravesend Bay were the waterside

accommodations of Bath Beach, Ulmer Park, and Bensonhurst-by-the-Sea. Elevated rapid transit, initially propelled by steam locomotives, connected the newly opened Brooklyn Bridge with the communities of East New York and Brownsville, and helped populate them.

Farther out on Long Island from Coney, ringing Jamaica Bay, were the sandy flats and brackish marshes of well-named Flatlands and the relatively virgin territory of New Lots. In the early thirties, Floyd Bennett Field was built on the wastes of barren Barren Island whose local industry transformed the corpses of horses into glue, soapfat, and fertilizer; no wonder the other side of Flatbush Avenue was given the name Dead Horse Inlet. Farther along the bay's shoreline lay two other waterfront communities: Bergen Beach and Canarsie Beach, each with its own early-1900s amusement facilities, which were considerably more provincial than those at Coney, and, being harder to get to, were tawdrier and less successful.

A number of related factors explain the growth of Brooklyn's fringe areas beginning in the early twenties. Expanding heavy industry, having completely occupied the lands closest to the harbor, started moving out to Queens or New Jersey. Although an idea to make Jamaica Bay a new Port of New York fizzled, light metals and chemicals, and the textile and apparel trades (none of which needed harbor or railroad access) moved farther into Brooklyn, encouraged by the city's new 1916 Zoning Law, which converted Brooklyn's older residential areas into commercial or unrestricted zones. Industry's intrusion was all the residents of

October 1933, saw a Hooverville of squatters' shacks in the vicinity of Columbia Street in Red Hook. In the distance is the Smith and Ninth Street IND viaduct and the spire of St. Mary's Star of the Sea Church, at Court and Luquer streets.

old Brooklyn needed when moving day rolled around. Rents were high everywhere, so why not move into modern accommodations, farther from Manhattan? With a small down payment (said the real estate ads), monthly charges would be no higher than rent. So they moved: "John, let's look somewhere else this time."

They looked in outer Brooklyn. The new zoning regulations declared the sections south of Brooklyn's glacial ridge as largely residential; not much industry would be making inroads there. The new subways—both the BMT routes to Coney Island and Bay Ridge, and the IRT extensions to Utica Avenue, New Lots, and along Nostrand Avenue—were making outer Brooklyn more accessible. The land was cheap. The recession after World War I persuaded state legislators to enact a five-year tax abatement for new housing. So speculators were building new places to live in, lots of them. (This was how Chanin Brothers, who would later build the Chanin Building, the Roxy and other Times Square theaters, and the Century and Majestic apartments on Central Park West, got their start, building small houses and apartment buildings in Bensonhurst.)

Between 1918 and 1929, 117,000 new residential structures were built in Brooklyn, 13,000 multiple dwellings, 58,000 two-family houses, and 46,000 individual homes. The vast majority were built in the communities of Brooklyn's fringe. The borough's housing boom was pulling many middle-class and lower-middle-class families to its frontiers, just as the post–World War II sub-

This ornate apartment building at 726 Ocean Avenue was still impressive in 1932, long after its movie star tenants, saddled with early morning calls at the nearby Vitagraph Studios, had vacated to Hollywood.

urban housing boom would draw many of them out of Brooklyn entirely, a generation or two later. Brooklyn became the mecca for the two-family house. "If the carrying charges are too high, rent the other unit and you'll be able to afford your own house."

Of course, municipal planning wasn't much more efficient then than it is now, even though your new home in Brooklyn's outer reaches might be near a trolley line or subway. (About 260 miles of subway were added citywide between 1914 and 1921.) In the latter year, almost half the land in Bensonhurst, Midwood, and Sheepshead Bay remained unimproved—no utilities, no sewers, sometimes not even any streets (except on the city map). In the decade between 1912 and 1922, Brooklyn increased its inventory of sewers from sixty miles to an astonishing 1,088. Yet it wasn't enough, nor were the sewage disposal facilities keeping up. Nevertheless, when city services did catch up, the residents had mixed feelings, for with the coming of asphalt and sewers came tax assessments aimed at paying for them.

Streets were widened. The eastern stretch of Kings Highway, for example, was made a true highway with median strips and all, not one in name only (which it had been since the days of the British). By December 1925, its wide swath was in place from Ocean to Flatbush Avenues. Completion from Flatbush to Howard Avenue and Eastern Parkway was promised "soon."

In the 1930s, Cropsey Avenue's widening would make access to Bensonhurst and Coney Island easier, while wiping out local New Utrecht landmarks like Texter's Ulmer Park Casino and "Con" Hogan's roadhouse at Harway Avenue and Bay 43rd. The picturesque old bridge over Coney Island Creek would be replaced as well. Emmons Avenue, the main drag along the north shore of Sheepshead Bay, would be rebuilt and widened, but that would wait until the mid-thirties and the WPA. That improvement wiped

The municipal ferryboat *Edward Riegelmann* awaits its load of black sedans seeking passage to the Rockaways at the bleak Jamaica Bay tip of Flatbush Avenue in the late twenties. No Kings Plaza then. The Coney Island Boardwalk is also officially named after Riegelmann, Brooklyn borough president in the years around World War I.

THE BAY PARKWAY STATIONS OF THE SEA BEACH AND WEST END SUBWAYS OF THE B. M. T.

THE LIBERAL TERMS OF SALE

$750.00 on account of the purchase price in cash, certified check, Liberty Bonds, Savings Bank Book, and the auctioneer's and salesroom fee of $23.00 at the time and place of sale.

MORTGAGES ON ALL HOUSES AS FOLLOWS

BAY PARKWAY

Nos. 7504, 7524, 7704

First Mortgage:—$8,500 at 6%, about 2¾ years to run, held by Title Guarantee & Trust Company.

Second Mortgage:—$6,000 at 6%, about 4 years to run, payable $225, quarterly.

Nos. 7416, 7420, 7508, 7512, 7516, 7520, 7708 and 7712

First Mortgage:—$8,000 at 6%, about 2¾ years to run, held by Title Guarantee & Trust Company.

Second Mortgage:—$5,500 at 6%, about 4 years to run, payable $225 quarterly.

No. 7624

First Mortgage:—$9,000 at 6%, about 2¾ years to run, held by Brevoort Savings Bank.

Second Mortgage:—$6,000 at 6%, about 4 years to run, payable $225 quarterly.

Nos. 7616 and 7620

First Mortgage:—$8,000 at 6%, about 2¾ years to run, held by Brevoort Savings Bank.

Second Mortgage:—$5,500 at 6%, about 4 years to run, payable $225 quarterly.

75TH STREET

Nos. 2138 to 2166

First Mortgage:—$7,000 at 6%, about 2¾ years to run, held by Title Guarantee & Trust Company.

Second Mortgage:—$4,500 at 6%, about 3¾ years to run, payable $200 quarterly.

76TH STREET

Nos. 2111 to 2163

First Mortgage:—$7,000 at 6%, about 2½ years to run, placed by New York Title and Mortgage Company.

Second Mortgage:—$4,500 at 6%, about 3¾ years to run, payable $200 quarterly.

Nos. 2114 to 2164

First Mortgage:—$7,000 at 6%, about 2½ years to run, placed by Lawyers Mortgage Company.

Second Mortgage:—$3,825 at 6%, about 3½ years to run, payable $175 quarterly.

77TH STREET

Nos. 2139 to 2169

First Mortgage:—$7,000 at 6%, about 2½ years to run, held by Kings County Savings Bank.

Second Mortgage:—$4,500 at 6%, about 3¾ years to run, payable $200 quarterly.

BALANCE OF THE PURCHASE PRICE, LESS THE MORTGAGES, TO BE PAID IN 30 DAYS FROM THE DAY OF SALE, ON DELIVERY OF THE DEED.

PUBLIC SCHOOL No. 186, A FEW BLOCKS FROM PROPERTY

HOW TO REACH THE PROPERTY

The B. M. T. Subway, either West End or Sea Beach Line to Bay Parkway, Station. Walk along Bay Parkway to property. A 5c bus line which runs along Bay Parkway and Kings Highway and connects with all subways passes this property at 77th Street.

out the jumble of waterside shacks and rotting piers, but it never restored the excitement of the yachts and other sailing craft that gathered there in the prosperity of the twenties' roar.

In those days an astonishing amount of land in Brooklyn's southern tier was still being used as farms—even dairy farms, like the one on Wortman Avenue, almost at the Queens border. It hung on until after World War II. As late as 1927 there was still a six-acre farm along Canarsie Lane, near the ancient Wyckoff homestead, in East Flatbush. The area around Kings County Hospital continued to be called "pig town" (for the small-scale undercover animal husbandry practiced there) until after the war, even though they were raising goats by then. And into the mid-fifties, two truck farmers, Philip Martino and Antonio Ossitti, raised seven acres of escarole and dandelion for Italian customers out on Flatlands Avenue and Ralph.

Some of the large acreage used for development came from the former racetracks of Kings County, doomed by reform governor Charles Evans Hughes's antigambling legislation in 1912. Sheepshead Bay Race Track, originally purchased from the wealthy Harkness interests for use in the sport of kings, was later sold for auto racing. In 1917, Harry S. Harkness bought the track back and renamed it the Harkness Motor Speedway. Racing cars weren't quite as popular as horses, though they were considerably noisier, and soon the speedway was in the hands of a syndicate headed by Max Nathanson, who auctioned it off in 20 × 100-foot lots along Ocean Avenue and 40 × 100 elsewhere. Some of the area actually

The piers along Sheepshead Bay were a tatty group before WPA entirely rebuilt the shoreline in the late thirties. But they had a nautical air and attracted some substantial yachts. Note the young man, in the foreground, hitching a bus ride on Emmons Avenue.

wasn't developed until the early 1950s, when the six-story Nostrand Gardens was built for returning veterans.

Another Nathanson sale was the Jamaica Bay frontage of old Bergen Beach, as well as its amusement park. Two thousand lots that he bought in February 1925 for $2 million were turned over for $2.5 million in December of that year.

Other acreage was in the hands of the Flatbush Water Works Company, which, in addition to supplying water, was in the business of banking land (fortunately for their stockholders, for the infamous taste of "Flatbush water" suggested that the company's days as a public utility were numbered). For decades the F.W.W.C. sold pieces of its extensive holdings to help straighten out the boundary lines of neighboring lots being offered by such developers as the Germania Real Estate and Improvement Company. As late as 1948, the water company's land was still being sold off for a sixty-one-building apartment project at Nostrand and Newkirk avenues.

One of Brooklyn's most unusual developments of the twenties was Gerritsen Beach, which fronts on Shell Bank Creek. The land, 1,100 lots, had been purchased for $300,000 by an Indiana land speculator who resold it in three years for twice the price. The new owners, Realty Associates, promising well-built, moderately

Antigambling legislation in 1912 ended horse racing at Brooklyn's three tracks. By 1914 the stands again filled at Brighton Beach Racetrack with people watching—and perhaps informally wagering on—auto races.

priced homes for wage earners, started the construction process on January 1, 1923. A suction dredge pumped 8,000 cubic yards of sand per day onto the marshy site until it was seven feet above mean high water. Then, after dredging a 1,700-foot-long canal and building roadways, curbs, and sidewalks, the company began house construction. On lots as tiny as 34 × 52.5 feet, and fronting on an alphabetized street system, 2,500 homes had risen by 1931. The modest wood-frame houses were protected against conflagrations by a volunteer fire company, today Brooklyn's only remaining one.

As each of the developments gained in population, it became evident that community organization would be the only effective means for securing necessary city services and improvements. The mid-twenties saw the emergence of the Marine Park Civic League, the Flatbush Square Civic Association, and the curiously titled Endocardium Community League in the East 50s from Avenue L to Avenue N.

Not only housing developments were under way; some attention was also being given to amenities. In 1911, Chicago's Daniel ("make no little plans") Burnham proposed some civic design reforms for Brooklyn, one being a new waterfront park on Jamaica Bay to complement the inland Prospect Park. Beginning with a gift in 1920 of 120 acres and $72,000 from Brooklyn philanthropists Frederic B. Pratt and Alfred T. White, holdings were accumulated until, by 1930, the city had spent $7 million to acquire 1,821 acres of what today is called Marine Park. (Included were the lands of philanthropist Harry Payne Whitney, which his father, Manhattan streetcar magnate William C. Whitney, had inherited from an old Brooklyn family, the Van Brunts.) In 1932, to mark the two-hundredth anniversary of George Washington's birth, and thereby to encourage the development of the park (which is still incomplete today) Congressman Sol Bloom suggested that a commemorative world's fair be built there. Instead, a copy of Mount

With time still on their hands at the end of the Depression, neighborhood "boys"—Fats, Chink, Mickey, Russo, and Benny—in South Brooklyn had just enough to do some good-natured horsing around for the Kodak Brownie, in 1939.

Vernon was temporarily erected—in Prospect Park—as a money-losing project of Grover Whalen, chairman of the celebration's Bicentennial Commission. Whalen used this valuable experience later, when running the 1939–40 World's Fair at Flushing Meadows. That one lost $200 million.

Not all development was new. Some settlements simply changed their character during this era. Blythebourne, an exclusive residential community, begun in 1887 at Thirteenth Avenue and Fifty-seventh Street, by 1921 had been completely swallowed up in the Borough Park neighborhood to the north and east, whose development was much less exclusive.

The Town of Gravesend, founded by English refugee Lady Deborah Moody (whose four central squares at the crossing of McDonald Avenue and Gravesend Neck Road represent one of America's oldest planned communities), ironically grew like Topsy. Advertising man Jerry Della Femina's 1978 book *An Italian Grows in Brooklyn* is unsurpassed in painting a sardonic picture of this area in the thirties and forties.

Bensonhurst attracted apartment buildings, some in the Art Deco style, as well as a wealth of all sorts of housing types. There, as well as in the other burgeoning communities, artfully crafted bank buildings were built at significant corners of the community. Thrift, after all, was what made it possible for the newcomers to settle here. Wise bankers saw in the new residents a source of income that would allow them to offer mortgages to others who would follow.

The BMT's Fourth Avenue subway reached Eighty-sixth Street in 1916, and Ninety-fifth Street in 1925. It spurred block after block of brick apartments along the broad avenues of Bay Ridge and Fort Hamilton that now found themselves only a nickel away from jobs in Manhattan. Apartments with names such as The Marlborough-Blenheim, The Chatelaine, and The Royal Poinciana were built along Fourth Avenue. Even during the Depression, construction continued in the form of Flagg Court, at Ridge Boulevard between Seventy-second and Seventy-third, the former site of Mr. Cocheau's Ridge Club. There, between 1933 and 1936, an imaginative and forward-looking apartment complex, complete with playhouse, swimming pool, and arcades, was erected from a design by innovative New York architect Ernest Flagg, whose accomplishments included Manhattan's Singer Tower.

Between 1921 and 1926, the waters lying below Shore Road were filled in by building a seawall and depositing earth excavated from the many nearby development sites. (The scene resembled a movie of the excavation of the Panama Canal, except that the film would have seemed to be running backwards.) The perimeter Shore Parkway, part of Robert Moses's Belt system, which, years later, was built on the filled land, opened on May 30, 1941, but had little effect on this area except to make it easier to bypass. The large homes and estates overlooking the harbor held on until after World War II, when those that were easily accessible to Shore Road fell, one by one, to development pressures. (Who the families are that still live in the remaining mansions, obscured from view atop Shore Road's lofty concrete and stone retaining walls,

The VITAGRAPH Co. of America

Rehearsing a Scene   Painting the Scenery

Making Projecting Machine

The Joining Room

Going out for a Big Scene

Wardrobe Department

If Brooklyn had had summertime weather all year round, the early Vitagraph Studios might have continued to produce movies near the Avenue M station of the Brighton Line. The structures are still there but successor Warner Brothers is in Hollywood.

remains a mystery to this day.) An exception was Fontbonne Hall Academy, run by the Sisters of Saint Joseph at 99th and Shore Road. It was originally the Robinson Estate and once the home of Lillian Russell. A less well-known occupant was Tom L. Johnson, the so-called Three-Cent Mayor of Cleveland, who lived there while he was a Brooklyn streetcar magnate. It was he who dropped the carfare from the Brooklyn Bridge to Coney Island from a quarter to a nickel in the 1890s, thus popularizing Coney among the masses. Johnson was a close friend and admirer of another Bay Ridge resident, single-taxer Henry George; they rest in adjacent graves at Greenwood Cemetery.

The whole center of new Brooklyn was distinguished most by its *allees* of trees. Planted at various times as saplings by developers and new homeowners, they thrived in Brooklyn's soil and their branches arched over the miles of flat-as-a-board parallel streets that composed Brooklyn's various gridirons. Whatever lack of imagination the repetitive tracts of housing revealed about their developers and designers, the trees are not part of the evidence.

Smack in the heart of lower Flatbush—or should one say Midwood, or Northern Kings Highway?—lay Brooklyn's own movie industry. The Vitagraph motion picture studios that date from the silent era still stand surrounding the intersection of Avenue M and East 15th Street, even though the industry, like the Dodgers many years later, was lured away by California's charms. In 1928, the invention of practical talkies established Vita*phone*, which continued to make Warner Brothers short subjects until 1939. After the war, with the coming of commercial television, the old sound stages were given a new life when NBC established a color TV studio there in 1952. Mary Martin performed her acclaimed "Peter Pan" on that TV stage.

Stars of the silent screen lived in the area, and America's great cartoonist Winsor McCay, the creator of *Little Nemo,* did animated films for Vitagraph and lived for more than a decade at 1901 Voorhies Avenue in the Sheepshead Bay area.

Some of outer Brooklyn had been converted from farmland to residential communities before the onset of the twenties, but not with the same explosive growth experienced during that decade. One such early settlement was Canarsie. Its pier on Jamaica Bay had been the place where passengers bound for the Rockaways would transfer from the 1860s steam train, the Brooklyn and

Pitkin Avenue, here looking east from Rockaway Avenue in the early thirties, was the glittery main drag when Brownsville was ninety-five percent Jewish: it had *the* restaurants, *the* cafeterias, and clothing stores of every description.

Rockaway Beach Railroad, to the cross-bay boat. Renamed the Canarsie Railroad in 1906, the route was linked in 1928 to the new BMT service connecting Manhattan's Fourteenth Street with Williamsburg and Bushwick. The tracks gashed a divider near Brownsville's boundary with East New York, and even traversed a grade crossing complete with flashing lights and descending striped gates—just like the country! At the last stop, a free transfer to the Jamaica Bay shore was available via a Toonerville-type trolley that took its own littered route through the tall grass, phragmites, and reeds to the beach and the White House Restaurant or the Golden City Amusement Park—at least until the latter burned down in 1934. The bucolic right-of-way lasted until late 1942 when the trolleys were shifted to streetcar tracks that ran down the center of adjacent Rockaway Parkway's pavement. While Canarsie's reputation was clouded for years—almost literally—by the nearby landfills (called "dumps" by everyone except government officials), the recreation pier remained popular, particularly after it was rebuilt under Robert Moses.

Brownsville and East New York had small urbanized settlements dating from the 1890s, and both areas saw an influx of new population and the development of their vacant lands following World War I. The area north of traditional Brownsville, along the slight glacial incline, was called Ocean Hill and was heavily settled by an Italian community, as were many parts of East New York.

Brownsville's vivid history is a history of intense Jewish settlement. Its main drag was the shopping street of Pitkin Avenue, a name pronounced by the locals with such a heavy Yiddish accent that the New England roots of East New York's 1835 founder, John R. Pitkin, disappeared in the borscht. Among Brownsville's notable physical landmarks were Betsy Head Swimming Pool, a

vast outdoor natatorium, the magnificent Loew's Pitkin, the Hopkinson and Parkway theaters, and the settlement-house buildings of the Hebrew Educational Society at Hopkinson and Sutter avenues. Retail landmarks included Stone Avenue, where tuxedos and wedding gowns filled the show windows, and Rockaway Avenue, where you went to buy "a bedroom set." The sensational bankruptcy of the Bank of United States in 1930 left another kind of landmark, its local branch, where many hardworking members of the needle trades (many of them thinking the bank's name meant official government sanction) had trustingly deposited—and lost—their hard-earned savings.

Brownsville was also known as a rough place. At least one public-school teacher called the community a "huge cesspool of illiteracy and hoodlumism." Lepke's Murder, Inc. was spawned in a candy store there. Yet the neighborhood was sympathetic to new social movements. Margaret Sanger opened the first birth-control clinic there in 1916. Socialist and American Labor Party candidates knew they could get elected from there.

It was also fertile soil for a whole school of American writers: Matthew Josephson, Henry Roth, Gerald Green, Murray Schisgal, Irving Shulman, Alfred Kazin, Norman Podhoretz. Kazin's twenties boyhood at 256A Sutter Avenue is evoked in his *A Walker in the City.* Podhoretz's upbringing at 2027 Pacific Street took place in the forties and is described in his book *Making It.* In that memoir he shares with his readers his experiences in a lower-class part of Brownsville while he was a member of the red-satin-jacketed Cherokees gang.

Irving Shulman's *The Amboy Dukes* fictionally chronicles another gang, this one on Amboy Street, and the process of growing up among Brownsville's postwar adolescents and young adults. When it appeared in 1947, the book became a best-seller, a popular work to a whole generation of New Yorkers, and a sexual primer for many adolescents in those prudish days.

The forties and fifties were times when Brooklyn began to beckon to writers—those raised there, such as playwright Arthur Miller, and strangers like Carson McCullers. The house of Miller's parents, at 1350 East 3rd Street, became the model for Willy Loman's in *Death of a Salesman.* McCullers lived at 7 Middagh Street in a house demolished to make way for the Brooklyn-Queens Expressway. It served, for a brief period, as the gathering place for a host of American writers, artists, and musicians:

W. H. Auden, Paul and Sally Bowles, Richard Wright, Oliver Smith, Aaron Copland, Leonard Bernstein, Marc Blitzstein, Anaïs Nin, and even Gypsy Rose Lee and Salvador Dali. In the early forties, Richard Wright wrote *Native Son* while living on Carlton Avenue and using the summit of Fort Greene Park as a place to write. Poet Marianne Moore lived nearby, at 260 Cumberland Street. Theatrical designer Oliver Smith later moved to the Brooklyn Heights house at 70 Willow Street, where writer Truman Capote would also reside. The Fulton Street building of the Ovington Studios offered studio space to a range of Brooklyn artists and writers (Norman Mailer wrote *Barbary Shore* there) and even to a Russian spy. Between 1943 and 1950, thrifty Dodgers president Branch Rickey was said to have lived in the ball team's office building at 215 Montague Street, although most accounts simply said "in Brooklyn Heights." After Rickey courageously broke baseball's color line by putting Jackie Robinson on the team in 1947, Robinson moved his family into 5224 Tilden Avenue, east of Holy Cross Cemetery. Dodgers fielder and manager Gil Hodges lived not too far away and is now buried in Holy Cross.

In addition to the celebrities drawn to Brooklyn in the years following World War II, there also were war veterans and their families seeking shelter. They found temporary quarters in Quonset hut communities, established overnight on city land that lay beyond the fringe of the borough's prewar development. The Paerdegat area, along Jamaica Bay, was one such location. It had been the site of the landfill operations for which adjacent Canarsie's reputation had suffered for so many years. Just try to buy a house there today for under a hundred-and-a-half!

To many of those who grew up in Brooklyn between the end of World War I and the departure of the Dodgers, their upbringing was intended to lead inevitably to their own departure. Some found it easy. Some necessary. Others, like Norman Podhoretz, found it difficult. His book *Making It* begins this way:

> One of the longest journeys in the world is the journey from Brooklyn to Manhattan—or at least from certain neighborhoods in Brooklyn to certain parts of Manhattan.

5

THE CULVER, THE SEA BEACH, THE CANARSIE LINE

 eginning in the twenties, the end of the workday meant that crowds of needle-trades workers would pour onto the Times Square BMT platform for the daily trip home to Brooklyn. The garment center was in the process of being reestablished in midtown, in the "Seventh Avenue District", as the Save New York Committee called it. The BMT station under Broadway between 40th and 42nd streets was convenient to the district. The new concentration of garment manufacturing in one place corresponded to a change in the living patterns of garment workers. They were starting to work in one place and live in another. For many, that other place was Brooklyn.

The BMT express trains heading for Coney Island would roar into the station with such frequency that straphangers didn't even mind the wait. There were, after all, three different expresses all running on the same track. (The Culver Line used the Brooklyn Bridge, and later the Nassau Street Loop.) Since this was an early stop, many had a good chance for a seat all the way home. Except for those who had recently moved to new apartments in Brighton Beach, few among the weekday crowds traveled the entire distance. Between the busy DeKalb Avenue station, built under Flatbush Avenue Extension, and their last stop at the Atlantic shore, the routes diverged to cover a wide area of Brooklyn. Depending upon what part of the borough they were headed for, the evening commuters would be looking to take the particular express that would get them closest to home.

The evening crush in 1940 at the Times Square BMT station shows commuters squeezing on for that trip back to Brooklyn. Practically everyone had a hat then, even the fellow in the foreground, a Jughead look-alike, from *Archie Comics,* wearing his father's recycled fedora.

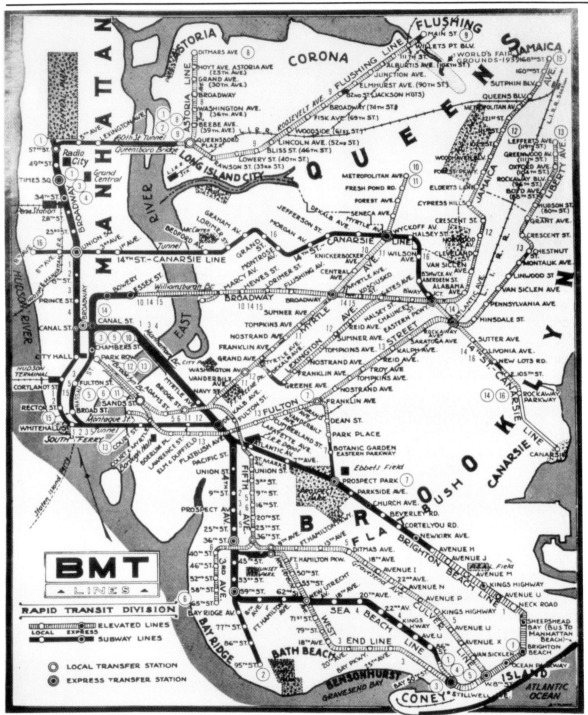

This mid-thirties BMT Lines route map shows the system when it was at its fullest. The Fulton Street, Lexington Avenue, and Myrtle Avenue els were still in operation. A route continued over the Brooklyn Bridge. The Fifth Avenue elevated branched out to a Third Avenue spur and also connected to the Culver Line to Coney Island.

Bunched together, the riders dared the platform's edge, those in front peering up the shiny tracks into the uptown darkness to see which express would be next. To make some order out of the chaotic scene, the BMT's management hung handmade wooden disks the size of pie plates from a cable over the heads of the crowd. The disks, of different colors, were neatly painted (when sign-painting was still an art) with the names of the three routes: BRIGHTON, SEA BEACH, WEST END. If you placed yourself under the disk marking the route you needed, the doors of your train—if the motorman had good aim in braking to a stop—would open in your vicinity. How civilized those disks were, and how civilized too were the names of the routes themselves.

True, they lacked the clipped preciseness of today's D, N, or B, the impersonal identities they've carried since 1967. But in comparison with today's information-theory pretentiousness, the old names on the disks had a certain charm, one that became part of many a Brooklynite's urban baggage. An important clue to who you were was where in Brooklyn you lived, and an important clue to where you lived was the route you took home.

Few remembered—or cared about—the origin of these names, which were carryovers from Brooklyn's one-time steam railroads, by then long forgotten. Anyway, many of the riders were recent emigrants to Brooklyn, interested not so much in the past as in the future. But the route names did have a comfortable ring to them.

The "Brighton Line," today's D train, derived from the Brooklyn, Flatbush and Coney Island Railway, which took its riders right up to the steps of the vast and fabled Brighton Beach Hotel. The "Culver Line" was nicknamed for its financier, Andrew Culver, whose Prospect Park and Coney Island Railroad followed a route that is largely that of today's F train. The "Sea Beach Line," which now carries the letter N, was originally the New York and Sea Beach Railroad, after its last stop, the Sea Beach Palace, a Coney Island amusement center. The last of the four, the "West End Line," now unceremoniously referred to as the B train, was the earliest of Brooklyn's steam roads. It began its career during the Civil War as the Brooklyn, Bath and Coney Island Railroad, but was later renamed the Brooklyn, Bath and West End to reflect the location of its terminal at the resort's west end; it was a name that took.

Even though the smoky engines and rustic wooden coaches out of a Buster Keaton epic were long gone, Brooklyn's old-timers

SEA BEACH LINE Now in Operation

Fastest and Finest Rapid Transit Railroad in the World.

THE SEA BEACH LINE to the ocean is now in operation in connection with the Fourth Avenue Subway. Service for the public was begun at 12 o'clock noon on Tuesday, June 22nd, trains operating from the Municipal Building station, Chambers Street and Park Row, Manhattan, to the Surf Avenue station (formerly West End terminal) in Coney Island.

Trains are running between Park Row and Coney Island on a four minute headway through the day and early evening, and making all stops at stations now open, they complete the trip to Coney Island in 41 minutes.

On days when conditions of travel justify it, an express service is operated which makes the trip from Park Row to Coney Island in 32 minutes.

Two hundred of the new subway cars of the New York Municipal Railway—cars 67 feet long and ten feet

Putting a new subway route into service meant the publication of a publicity puff piece extolling the merits of the new line. The New York Municipal Railway was one of the BMT's predecessors in the era before 1921.

were happy that the upgraded and electrified subway lines continued to carry the historic nicknames they always used.

During the time of the First World War, the four routes were being rebuilt. By decade's end the last of these Coney Island-to-Manhattan trunk lines had been completed. On August 1, 1920, the new subway portion of the Brighton Line, stretching beneath Flatbush Avenue's pavements from the Prospect Park station to the new six-track complex at DeKalb Avenue, was put into service. The new leg gave people living along the Brighton route a direct connection to midtown, and even made Lower Manhattan more convenient, adding new stops along Broadway. No longer would they have to take the old route: first to Franklin Avenue (using the same route that the Brighton shuttle still takes) and then along the rooftop route of the Fulton Street el. Finally, over the Brooklyn Bridge, and into the congested Park Row station at City Hall—the line's first, last, and only stop in Manhattan.

It was about time, Brighton Liners thought. Elsewhere in Brooklyn the previous five years had brought their neighbors significant improvements in service to "the city," which is how just about everyone referred to Manhattan. Travelers on Brooklyn's other three express lines out of Coney had already been provided a rapid, dependable trip to Manhattan, without even a change of trains. Using routes that newly converged under Brooklyn's broad Fourth Avenue, passed under downtown Brooklyn, and then crossed the Manhattan Bridge, they could easily reach the Canal Street station, which wasn't very far from the City Hall area served by the old Brooklyn Bridge trains. And by the late summer of 1917, the Manhattan Bridge service had even been extended

The Brighton Line under Flatbush Avenue was started and completed while the Brooklyn Public Library headquarters at Grand Army Plaza languished since its start of construction in 1912. The remnant, shown in 1930, was finally demolished in favor of a new structure, finished in 1941.

up Broadway to midtown, by July of 1919 reaching Fifty-seventh Street at Carnegie Hall.

The same August day in 1920 that marked the opening of the new Brighton Line also marked the opening of two new BMT subway tunnels under the East River. The Sixtieth Street Tunnel gave the uptown end of the BMT system access to Long Island City's Queensboro Plaza. More important to Brooklynites, however, was the Montague Street Tunnel, which made it easier to reach jobs at Manhattan's toe.

With these improvements in service, the BMT's empire was expanding, and with it Brooklyn's population would expand as well. Coincidental to the BMT's expansion, the IRT was also extending new branches into Brooklyn. Although it took until 1922 for its New Lots leg to be completed, the part traversing Eastern Parkway to Utica Avenue was also opened to traffic in 1920, as was the Nostrand Avenue spur to what the signs called Vandeveer Park.

The wall ad "Boyshform Diafram Brassiere" dates this view of Fulton and Gold streets as the early twenties when flat-chestedness for women was in vogue. The site to the east would soon be cleared for the RKO Albee Theatre, since replaced by the Albee Square Mall.

The expansion of the subway lines in the twenties is almost always viewed from the point of view of Manhattanites—how the new routes further strengthened the convenience and supremacy of the city's core. But what of their significance to Brooklynites, to the people who lived in the areas that the new extensions would now make more accessible to the core?

The expansion of Brooklyn's—and the city's—rapid transit began with the signing of the so-called Dual Contracts on March 19, 1913. The agreements called for a total of 620 miles of new trackage, a significant increase from the 296 then in existence. Out of that effort came the expansion of both existing subway systems—the IRT, the Interborough Rapid Transit Company, and the other that shortly would become known as the BMT, the Brooklyn-Manhattan Transit Company. In 1920 the latter was still called the BRT, the Brooklyn Rapid Transit Company. The change would come three years later from the BRT's bankruptcy, caused by the catastrophic 1918 wreck in the tunnel under Malbone Street (quickly renamed Empire Boulevard) on today's Franklin Avenue shuttle route. Close to 100 people were killed and over 250 injured, resulting in so many damage suits that the BRT was forced out of business. Its remains were reconstituted as the BMT.

The coming of all the new and extended routes not only contributed heavily to the exponential expansion of Brooklyn's residential

The arched station structure of the IND subway over Fourth Avenue at Ninth Street, here shown under construction, is reminiscent of parts of the Paris Metro's elevated sections. The station was opened on October 7, 1933.

Times Plaza, Junction of Atlantic and Flatbush Aves., Brooklyn, N. Y.

Subway and Elevated Stations, Coney Island, N. Y.

population, but also helped to make Manhattan more the center of many Brooklynites' lives. Already, many Brooklynites had jobs in Manhattan, either downtown or in the rapidly growing midtown, many drawn there, as we have seen, by the establishment of the new Garment Center. The strings of chocolate-brown-painted steel subway cars that rolled across Brooklyn's flats not only made Coney Island's beaches and amusements more accessible to everyone on hot summer weekends, they made Manhattan's Canal Street, Union Square, Herald Square, and Times Square more accessible to Brooklyn residents all the year round.

As the uptown BMT expresses crossed the East River over the Manhattan Bridge to continue their trip under busy Broadway, they began to shift the eating, shopping, and entertainment habits of large parts of Brooklyn's population. A cheap meal in an authentic Chinatown eatery or at a clam bar in Little Italy was only a nickel subway ride away, and a fairly rapid one at that. Similarly, retail shopping was no longer confined to a local dry-goods store or to a department store in downtown Brooklyn. Housewives could almost as easily shop for bargains on Fourteenth Street at "S. Klein on the Square" or at Ohrbach's, which opened diagonally across the intersection in 1923. And farther uptown were Macy's, Saks 34th Street, and Gimbel's, as well as the center of New York's night life and entertainment, which, by then, began a few blocks north at the Metropolitan Opera House and stretched to the far end of Times Square.

While Brooklyn was served in the twenties by two rapid transit systems, the IRT had less romance than the BMT, which ran three—count 'em, three—rapid transit empires: the overhead elevated system that dated from the nineteenth century, the new subways of the 1920s, and a complicated streetcar network through what seemed every major street. The IRT had only one system in the borough, primarily below ground, with essentially one kind of car. It was made of steel, totally enclosed, with rattan seats, some of which could be folded down across the car's center doors to make more seating space. White porcelained poles and overhead handgrips helped riders deal with unexpected starts and stops and sharp curves. In the early years the cars were regularly repainted, even to the decorative striping along the interior. But the layers of paint began to build up and the colors became muddier. Eventually every surface inside and out—except the white ceiling—became a gruesome olive drab enamel, like a vehicle of war rather than one of public transport.

A few features distinguished these IRT cars from the BMT's: they were shorter and narrower—only nine feet wide—and so had no room for the BMT-type three-plus-two crosswise seating where boyfriend and girlfriend could nuzzle. Instead the IRT cars had the same two ranks of seats grimly facing one another that they do today. The cars differed, too, in that they had recessed vestibules at each end that could be converted—in a few seconds—into motormen's cabs. More frequently, however, the niches served another purpose, to allow standing couples to steal a few hugs while they enjoyed some privacy from the eyes of the other riders, important in an era when everyone rode the subways and fewer had access to cars.

Destinations could be determined only from markers on the sides of the cars; these were signs painted in white on heavy black iron plates that were hung one below the other across the upper half of a window. Extra signs denoting other routes were kept in a metal box just underneath, their index tabs sticking up just high enough so that a conductor could read the abbreviations they bore. The front of the train carried no destination markings, unless you could figure out the color codes of the pair of signal lamps on the roof. Few did, apart from the IRT's towermen and dispatchers, for whose information they were really provided.

Unlike today, the entrances to the IRT cars back then had only one wide door per opening instead of a pair of narrower ones. Over the door windows was a spring clip to hold, when necessary, a simple cardboard sign that read DOOR OUT OF SERVICE. (It was rarely needed then; today, no clip, no sign, both badly needed.) The door's leading edge had a wide black rubber bumper, placed

there to prevent injury to last-minute climbers-aboard and to enclose a device that, when pressed, totally reversed the direction
of that closing door, thus reinitiating the door-closing cycle. This
was often a cue to other late arrivers to try to squeeze on: another
tap and the door opened wide again, and again. Truants, toughs,
and those with time on their hands would stand in the doorways
and rile harried conductors—and riders late for work—by repeat-
edly tapping the bumper into action. It could be a real pain.

To kids riding the subways, the IRT cars had other attractions.
Over the vestibule was a bell and clapper that was meant to convey signals by a tug on a woven maroon lanyard that snaked
through the cars. It dated from the days when a team of conductors planted their shoes on the projecting "fly parts" in the space
between cars to operate levers that opened and closed the doors
(trains were much shorter then). They yanked the lanyards to
pass along the word to the next conductor (and ultimately the
motorman) that the doors were safely closed and that the train
could proceed. By the twenties, the bells and signal cords were
still in good order but rarely yanked.

The vestibule also offered front-car riders a hand-brake wheel,
useful for young riders to "steer" the train through the labyrinthine
tunnels. And, next to the wheel, there was a curious black board
with one wedge-shaped end (officially called a "slipper," but who
knew that?). Slipped between the electrified third rail and the
subway car's contact shoe in time of emergency, this isolated the
car from its power system. Often, however, its unintended use
was as the motorman's weapon of defense against hooligans.

Last, there was that mysterious steel box with curved top and
bottom, fastened overhead to the back of the vestibule bulkhead.
It had a keyhole guarded by a brass escutcheon. This, too, seemed
not to serve a significant purpose except that sometimes at the
end of a run the motorman could be spied inserting a key, causing
a strip of paper to emerge, as from an adding machine, which he
tore off and stuffed into his pocket. In fact the box contained a
recorder that measured the distance the train had coasted on that
shift. What with the nickel fare and the need to show a profit, the
IRT's management sought whenever possible to run its trains the
natural way, using gravity and momentum whenever possible, instead of costly electric power. To underscore this policy, the
IRT's motormen were therefore required to turn in their coasting
records regularly.

The BMT's sixty-seven-foot-long steel subway cars, with three pairs of doors on each side (rather than the IRT's stingy three singles), were more reminiscent of the ones in use on the London Underground than anything previously seen in the New York vicinity. As in London, the conductor opened the train's doors from the inside, where he stood among his passengers, and not from the unprotected spot between the cars, to which the IRT relegated its personnel. Having opened the doors, the BMT conductor stepped partway out of his doorway in the middle of the center car and, with fingers poised on a row of buttons set into a brass plate, "touch-typed" them closed, first those to his right, then those to his left, and finally the ones he himself was using, at which point he'd buzz the motorman that it was safe to go. *Brrrp. Brrrp.*

Discontinuance of elevated service was sometimes greeted with glee. Here a group of Pratt Institute faculty celebrates the last ride on the Lexington Avenue el between Gates and Myrtle avenues on October 13, 1950.

These cars, called "standards," had a design that brought dignity to the Brooklynites' commute. They rode more smoothly, ran more quietly, and their greater width of ten feet permitted L-shaped seating arrangements that allowed for single riders as well as family groups to be comfortably accommodated. As in the IRT, the seats were of rattan the color of woven wheat.

But in addition to the stately steel cars that had been designed to negotiate the new subway tunnels, the BMT also had an enormous array of antiquated cars left over from the nineteenth century. These were lightweight wooden coaches—nine feet wide, like the IRT's—that had loped along Brooklyn's elevateds ever since 1885, the year Brooklyn's first, the "Old Main Line," started running along Lexington Avenue to East New York. (Yes, Brooklyn has a Lexington Avenue, too.) The elevated cars boasted open platforms with wire-mesh gates. This gave them the look of observation cars, the kind that presidents used for whistle-stop speeches, only the BMT's were double-ended. While they were no fun for the conductors who had to open the gates by hand, regardless of how cold or rainy it was, they were great fun for passengers in the warm months, when it was possible to ride the windswept platforms of the gate-fronts over the streets of Brooklyn and watch the bedroom windows and rooftops zip by. As the years passed, these gate-front cars were either assigned just to rush-hour service or, even worse, rebuilt so as to enclose their open platforms, as though to eliminate their special capacity to engender fun.

The elevated cars were not only older and shorter than the steel ones, but narrower and lighter, so as not to exceed the load capacity and clearances of the old viaducts that cast latticed shadows along Brooklyn's streets. As more and more of the heavier and wider cars were added to the subway fleet, connections were made between the below-ground routes and some of the elevated lines, whose weight-bearing capacity was then beefed up. Station platforms were also shaved to accommodate the wider cars. To bridge the resulting gap when the nine-foot-wide elevated cars were in use at platforms cut back for ten-foot clearances, BMT's clever maintenance forces designed threshold extensions and sloping sills for the older cars that further added to their distinctive appearance.

The ingenuity and forward-looking character of the BMT's management showed itself in other ways. In 1927 it introduced the "D-type" articulateds, three-car units that shared only four sets of wheels and made it possible for riders to move from one car to the next through little vestibules that eliminated that between-the-cars gap and those scary looks down onto the open tracks speeding by below. To substitute for the old wooden cars on the elevateds, a couple of five-unit experimental, lightweight, metal-skinned articulateds were put into service in 1934. One was the Budd Company's stainless-steel Zephyr, featuring red leather seats and a fancy braking system. The other was the Pullman Company's advanced design Duralumin train, labeled the Green Hornet. (Others called it the Blimp, for all those rounded corners it sported.) Among its features were chimes to signal the closing of doors, electric-eye-controlled lights that automatically turned on in tunnels and off in daylight, and other foretastes of the future.

In 1939, just one year before it was absorbed into a unified municipally owned and managed system, the BMT introduced its new three-unit Bluebird train—another articulated—this one warmly received by the riding public. Before the city's timid Board of Transportation could intervene, five more units of cars were

Subway posters like this one helped develop support for the $500 million bond issue that voters approved in November 1951. It paid for the promised improvements under DeKalb Avenue and for others. But the Nostrand and Utica avenues extensions were never even begun.

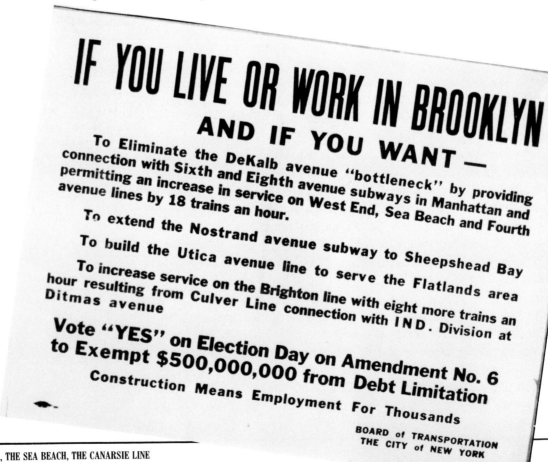

IF YOU LIVE OR WORK IN BROOKLYN
AND IF YOU WANT —

To Eliminate the DeKalb avenue "bottleneck" by providing connection with Sixth and Eighth avenue subways in Manhattan and permitting an increase in service on West End, Sea Beach and Fourth avenue lines by 18 trains an hour.

To extend the Nostrand avenue subway to Sheepshead Bay

To build the Utica avenue line to serve the Flatlands area

To increase service on the Brighton line with eight more trains an hour resulting from Culver Line connection with IND. Division at Ditmas avenue

Vote "YES" on Election Day on Amendment No. 6
to Exempt $500,000,000 from Debt Limitation

Construction Means Employment For Thousands

BOARD of TRANSPORTATION
THE CITY of NEW YORK

added. Built by a newcomer to the field, the Clark Equipment Company of Battle Creek, Michigan (no, Virginia, they weren't shot from guns), these streamlined, blue-hued trains used state-of-the-art wheel trucks developed for the esteemed PCC trolley, the Presidents Conference Committee car, the first of which had also been tested in Brooklyn a few years earlier. The PCC was designed to overcome the deficiencies of American trolleys as determined by tests performed—where else?—on Brooklyn's trolley tracks in the early thirties. Using their voluminous findings and a war chest provided by the presidents of twenty-five American streetcar companies, a team of experts developed the streamlined PCC trolley car that, in 1985 at least, is still seeing service in San Francisco, Pittsburgh, Philadelphia, Boston, and Newark . . . but not in Brooklyn. The PCC, as well as the other innovative rapid transit ideas, the Bluebird, the Green Hornet, the Zephyr, and the D-type articulateds, have all been retired—meaning all have been scrapped, both the cars and the imaginative concepts they first suggested for better mass transit.

Let us rather look at the brighter side: diesel fumes, the Grumman Flxible, graffiti.

Trolley 1039 was one of Brooklyn's modern fleet of PCC cars, evolved through tests conducted partly on Brooklyn streets. Here it waits on the Brooklyn Bridge alongside a line of sedans on their way into lower Manhattan in 1938.

6

THEY CAME FROM EVERYWHERE

n the distance, running alongside Linden Boulevard atop a dark embankment, were the tracks of an anonymous railroad line, together with a miscellany of dusty freight cars parked at a siding. They recalled one of twentieth-century Brooklyn's few vestiges of its iron-horse past, something we knew about only vicariously, through the chugging images in the second-feature B-Westerns viewed at the obligatory Saturday matinees of our youth. But this railroad was steam no longer; its fussy strands of overhead wires told the story. Boxy electric engines—looking nothing like the locomotives in the movies—hummed and buzzed as they shunted strings of freightcars back and forth. Actually, they were moving freight from harborside piers at Sixty-ninth Street into the depths of Brooklyn and farther out on Long Island, into Queens, Nassau, and Suffolk.

Fascinating as it was for kids to watch the pantographed locomotives maneuver the earth-colored boxcars, hoppers, and gondolas back and forth under the high-voltage wires, it was what lay on the other side of the earthen barrier that was even more intriguing. The tall embankment separated two communities, East Flatbush on the north and Canarsie on the south. And, depending upon which side you lived on, the other seemed alien, different. Jews, for the most part, lived in East Flatbush. Canarsie, on the other hand, was then primarily an Italian enclave. Both communities owed their respective demographic textures to the tides of immigration that had been washing America's shores for decades.

It wasn't very difficult to tell which of the neighborhoods you

The men and boys of the parish have for decades carried the five-story-high *giglio* (lily) through the streets of their Williamsburg neighborhood in the height of midsummer heat to mark the feasts of Our Lady of Mt. Carmel and St. Paulinus of Nola.

Row houses along a typical street in East Flatbush in the 1950s. Curb space was hard to find by then, so a built-in garage was handy—as was the income that came from the resulting ground floor–rear apartment.

were in. East Flatbush reflected the concerns of those who remembered their own early years in the small towns of "the Pale"—in Eastern Poland and the Ukraine—or could recall the stories they had been told by their parents or grandparents of life "on the other side," in Europe. East Flatbush was not a very green place. Whatever open space remained around the brick or stucco row houses of the area after the developers had departed was largely paved concrete sidewalk or driveway. The patches of grass, too small to dignify with the name "lawn," hardly justified the purchase of a mower—sometimes neighbors would chip in to share one. So it came as no surprise that Italian masons were soon called in by the Jewish residents to close off the meager weedy patches with pink-toned cement, often scored in swirling or flag-stone-like patterns.

In contrast, Canarsie was an agricultural wonderland, at least for a place well within the boundaries of a large American city. Here, on flats that dampened and became brackish and boggy as they approached Jamaica Bay, one found an array of greenery that overgrew the frame houses and sent out visual signals of a rural farm community, despite its nearness to Manhattan. The undeveloped plots burst forth every summer with lush crops of tomatoes, arugula, grapes—whatever could prosper in Brooklyn's climate and could recall memories of a peasant childhood in southern Italy and Sicily. Goats and other livestock, though technically prohibited by law, were not exactly unknown. In Canarsie's harsh winters, the landscape assumed a striking appearance, the soil turning gray and the remains of last year's crops adding a melancholy paleness. Wreaths of grapevines clung to primitive wooden arbors. One saw, huddled in side yards, the gnarled black sculptures of tar-papered fig trees, each capped against winter's rains and snows by an upended tin bucket, the branches within gathered together at the onset of frost against the biting salt-soaked winds from the nearby bay.

Canarsie, despite its distinctive Amerindian name, sent out the muted message of a Mediterranean landscape and a people whose hands were callused from years spent tilling the soil. East Flatbush, however, showed a different strain, reflecting the concerns of the *shtetl,* the trades and crafts and domestic pursuits of the villages and hamlets that dotted the Eastern European plains. One community echoed the fields, the other the town.

The dividing lines of Brooklyn's ethnic communities were not always as bold on the horizon as the railroad embankment dividing Canarsie from East Flatbush. Nor were the streetscapes of other communities always so ethnically informative. Nevertheless, ethnic epicenters dotted Brooklyn, sometimes corresponding neatly to neighborhood identities, but ofttimes not. The idea that the people in this melting pot lived happily with one another in a pastel fairyland was hardly borne out by the bloody noses of kids who voyaged into someone else's turf, or by walls bearing chalked

Italian neighborhoods, like Canarsie or East New York, often overflowed with verdant gardens. The IRT New Lots elevated is visible, in the distance, in this 1934 view of a whole block full of gardens along Ashford Street, north of Linden Boulevard, in East New York.

testimony to hostilities that raged long before the spray can was invented. Mick. Sheeny. Wop. Nigger. Polack. Spic. Or D.T.K.L.A.M.F., which translated as "Down to Kill Like A Mother Fucker." And as rich in ethnic diversity as neighborhoods could be, the different groups didn't really encourage too much mixing. For every Abie's Irish Rose you could name, there were at least two houses draped in black for sons and daughters who had married out of the faith, and were considered by their families to be dead.

The Irish had come early, beginning with the potato famine in 1845. By the twenties and beyond, they had grown large in number and in political power and had spread widely throughout much of the city. The area below the Navy Yard, the southern reaches of Park Slope, as well as Windsor Terrace, Sheepshead Bay, and Gerritsen Beach had particularly strong pockets, but as one looks through the records of the Brooklyn Archdiocese, it is evident that in the period before and after World War II it was the sons of Irish Catholic families who predominated in Church functions, and that throughout the length and breadth of the borough, Irish priests and monsignors had a particularly important role in Brooklyn's Catholic parishes, whatever their ethnic allegiance.

Until the early twenties, Brooklyn was a Republican stronghold. Places like South Flatbush continued to give their votes to the GOP in national and congressional elections until as late as 1926. But in 1927 the Democratic Party took a clean sweep of all borough offices, and John H. McCooey, the local Democratic leader since 1909, reflecting Kings County's traditional Irish strength, was crowned "King of Kings."

Memories of life "on the other side" sometimes took form in primitive paintings on the walls of Brooklyn's business establishments, like this poultry market at North Fourth and Roebling streets in Williamsburg, shown in 1941.

Jews first entered Brooklyn when the 1800s were turning into the 1900s. They were seduced by dreams of escape from the poverty of Manhattan, by alluring descriptions of Brownsville and East New York, and by the easy walk from their Lower East Side "old law" tenements across the bridge into Williamsburg. (The bridge soon became "Jew's Bridge" in the hands of the city's not very friendly newspapers.) By the mid-twenties the Jewish emigration into Brooklyn had caused the biggest change in the com-

Hundreds of Brooklyn's Roman Catholics paid a visit to Borough Hall Plaza to honor Holy Year in 1950. Fulton Street, on the right, is minus its elevated but the future site of the State Supreme Court building is still filled with miscellaneous shops.

As much as Brooklyn was known for its abundant street life, celebrations in Momma's kitchen were also an important part of life as this 1945 scene shows. Oilcloth covered the table and lots of big serving bowls provided plenty of food for everyone.

position of Brooklyn's foreign-born population. Like banners of an invading army, there appeared all over Brooklyn silver-and-black signs hand-painted on the plate-glass windows of kosher butchers: "boh-*sor* ko-*sher*"—kosher meat. In the years following World War I, over a third of all foreign-born people moving to Brooklyn were Jews who had come from Russia and Poland. Many moved into Brownsville, but the more adventurous sought homes in places like Crown Heights, Bedford-Stuyvesant, even parts of Flatbush and Borough Park, and, of course, Brighton Beach and environs.

The Williamsburg community, which had offered a new opportunity to Jews after 1903, proved to be a promised land again, this time to a second wave of Jews, various sects of Chasidim who began to settle there in the turbulent years prior to America's entry into World War II. Following the end of the war, these groups, now well known through Chaim Potok's books and the film adaptation of his novel *The Chosen,* increased their numbers in Brooklyn, as those who had survived the Holocaust made their way across the ocean. While groups known as the Satmarer, the Stolin-Karliner, and the Tzelemer—after the European communities they were forced to flee—remained in Brooklyn, the Vishnitzer moved to suburban Rockland County, and the adherents of the Skvarer *rebbe* to nearby New Square, a community they founded. The title "New Jerusalem" has been used in connection with Williamsburg, Borough Park—another Chasidic enclave—and, before them, Brownsville.

One of Brooklyn's more colorful political leaders in the first half of the twentieth century was Hymie Schorenstein, Brownsville's Democratic boss. He initially achieved his fame for having coaxed Brownsville's Jewish population away from the Socialists, who enjoyed a strong following among the laboring classes after the First World War. For his efforts he was awarded the paid position of county Commissioner of Records, a post it turned out he was able to handle despite his being unable to read or write. He seemed always caught without his eyeglasses when called upon to engage in either skill. Not having to waste his time with the written word, Schorenstein chose to use his time thinking about things. To him is credited by some—*Bartlett's Familiar Quotations* to the contrary notwithstanding—the journalistic aphorism, "Dog bites man—that ain't news. Man bites dog—*that's* news!"

Brooklyn's German community was best known for having established a widely admired array of breweries in the late nineteenth century. So it was no surprise that those areas where the aroma of malt and hops filled the air—Bushwick, Ridgewood, and East Williamsburg—were also the homes of many a German family. Carrying their European values to Brooklyn, the Germans scrubbed their neighborhoods until they positively glistened. It was an everyday occurrence to find an army of *hausfraus* washing stoops and sidewalks with water so hot it steamed into the cool morning air. The novelist Henry Miller, born in Manhattan, was brought to Williamsburg in his first year and lived there between 1892 and 1913, when it was heavily German. He first lived at 622 Driggs Avenue, and then on Decatur Street between Bushwick and Evergreen Avenues, which he dubbed his "Street of Early Sorrows."

Airplanes weren't all that prevalent in Brooklyn's skies in 1939 but this lucky tyke had one of her own, with a two bladed propellor and an air-cooled radial engine, too—or a reasonable facsimile of one.

The distinctive five onion domes of the Russian Orthodox Cathedral of the Transfiguration, overlooking McCarren Park, mark large eastern European settlements in both Greenpoint and Williamsburg.

Brooklyn's Jewish community was represented architecturally with a vast array of synagogues and *talmud torahs* (Hebrew schools), which dotted many of Brooklyn's neighborhoods. This photo was taken on Mermaid Avenue and Beach 23rd Street.

The maritime trades brought the Scandinavians. Ships' carpenters, seamen, longshoremen, they planted their families on the uplands along Buttermilk Channel and Upper Bay, behind the docks and warehouses that formed Bush Terminal. Before the end of mass European immigration, in 1924, the harbor end of Atlantic Avenue was known as Swedish Broadway. Beginning in 1890, Finns settled around Sunset Park, which they knew as Pukinmäki, Goat Hill. To maximize their limited economic resources, families pooled their savings and in the 1910s and 1920s built New York's first true cooperative apartment houses developed upon working-class economic principles they had learned in Scandinavia. Along Fifth Avenue and down into Bay Ridge there were newsstands selling the Norwegian *Nordiske Tidende* as well as newspapers meant for the local Danes, Finns, and Swedes. Food shops appeared that prepared the special foods of the fair-skinned, fair-haired northern Europeans who settled along the area's side streets: Fredericksen and Johannesen, Hinrichsen's, the Heise deli, Lund's, Olsen's, and Leske's.

Stores with signs reading LATTICINI FRESCHI, displaying cheeses and smoked hams hanging from overhead racks, and pork stores bearing noticeably Italian names—Salvatore's, Tony's, Mario's—announced neighborhoods heavy with Brooklyn's considerable Italian population. With the rise in economic status of the sons and daughters of immigrants, many—though not all—of Italian extraction started moving from places like Greenpoint and Williamsburg, South Brooklyn and Gowanus to new two-family and private homes in Bensonhurst, Bath Beach, East New York, and other perimeter communities. All over Brooklyn could be found parishes named for Italian saints: St. Francis of Paola, St. Blaise, St. Lucy (not Santa Lucia, mind you), St. Rita, St. Rocco, St. Rosalia. Other parishes carried Italian names celebrating the Virgin Mary: Our Lady of Loretto, Our Lady of the Rosary of Pompeii, and many, many others.

Onion-domed churches that enriched the skylines of Greenpoint

Everyone, regardless of age or gender, turned out to wish the boys in uniform good luck. The main street of the neighborhood, in this case Court Street, was the site of victory parades.

Frame houses from the thriving nineteenth-century black community of Weeksville appear in this ca. 1920 photograph. They still stand (now restored) along old Hunterfly Road, off Bergen Street between Rochester and Buffalo avenues. St. Mary's Hospital is in the background.

and East New York marked Ukrainian communities. St. Stanislaus Kostka and Our Lady of Czestochowa churches meant that Polish Catholics lived in concentration in Brooklyn, too. There was even a sizable French community in Brooklyn then—served by the Roman Catholic Church of St. Louis at Ellery Street near Nostrand Avenue.

While technically not an ethnic group, Brooklyn's black community, like every other in a predominantly white society, was a particularly visible one, even though numerically quite small in those days. Nineteenth-century blacks had established a few communities—with names like Carrsville and Weeksville—in what whites snidely came to call Crow Hill, now the northern part of Crown Heights. By the 1920s and early thirties, a linear community had begun to form between the grimy shadows of the Fulton Street elevated and the Long Island Rail Road's viaduct along Atlantic Avenue, a settlement that later grew to become America's largest black community, Bedford-Stuyvesant. During World War II and afterward, the by-now dilapidated turn-of-the-century frame tenements near Livonia Avenue's IRT elevated in Brownsville—housing that been a haven to the early Jewish migrants from Manhattan—started to be exploited as rentals for poor blacks who had few options as to where they could live.

The tide of Puerto Rican settlement came after World War II, when *barrios* grew in parts of Williamsburg and South Brooklyn.

Holiday parades brought out the American Legion and the Jewish War Veterans—and the politicians. Every parish had a parade on its respective saint day. Parochial-school bands with smartly uniformed proto-teenagers marched in step, playing painfully rehearsed martial music. These events annually formed a graphic index to the complexity of ethnic life in the borough. The big-bosomed representatives from the nurses' corps, proudly strutting along with the veterans, never failed to surprise, what with the preponderance of uniformed men in the ranks.

Election days were invariably followed by community bonfires, started either in vacant lots or on the streets. What the garbage men failed to pick up became the fuel for the celebratory pyres. The winners of the citywide or national contests were sometimes undetermined until the next day, but the local candidates were always a shoe-in and their victory an invariable cause for celebration.

Between the twenties and the fifties, when vacant lots could still be found in Brooklyn, the warm-weather months couldn't go by without the appearance of at least one carnival, a block party. They weren't very impressive in the daytime, but once the sun set, the lights and motion and smells and rides made them mini–Coney Islands. Sponsorship as part of the local parish bazaar made gambling okay, and so the other sounds of the night were joined by the incessant *ticky-ticky-ticky* spins of the wheels of chance. One of the most spectacular celebrations has taken place every July since the early 1900s in the area around Havemeyer Street and Union Avenue in Williamsburg. The men of the community, descendants of settlers from the village of Nola, outside Naples, traditionally carry a five-story-high decorated tower of enormous weight called the *giglio,* the lily, through the streets of their neighborhood. The "dancing of the *giglio*" celebrates St. Paulinus's rescue of their ancestral village in A.D. 485. Added to the spinning games of chance, the steaming sausage, and all the other ingredients of a church bazaar, the event sums up the richness of Brooklyn's ethnicity.

7

MINE WAS THE BEST BLOCK

As different as each Brooklyn neighborhood was, what really stood out in your memory was the block you were raised on.

When crossing the street meant holding somebody else's hand—"Cross me, mister?"—the block was the space inside its curbs. With time, it grew to become both sides of the street, and to include the gutter—where school teachers and Hollywood's do-good movies said you'd wind up if you didn't behave yourself.

The whole world radiated from that piece of turf called "my block." The rest was characterized by such expressions as "around the corner" or "over by the lots" (empty, back then), or "in the schoolyard."

The block had its separate parts. Closest, of course, was the building where you grew up. For those who lived on Brooklyn's outskirts, home meant a private house. But for most Brooklynites, home was some kind of multiple dwelling: a two- or four-family house, a walkup, a tenement, or, with the coming of the 1930s, a six-story elevator apartment. Those often had a sunken living room and streamlined brickwork, chrome-plated zigzags on the lobby doors, and fancy decoration where the walls met the sky. Depending on what the zoning called for and the price the developer paid for the land—or sometimes on the whim of an architect or builder—these housing units wound up surrounded by some kind of open space. If you were lucky, there was a fragment of lawn and maybe a concrete alley to run along on the way to the garage in back. Some of the apartment buildings were wrapped

Fellas and gals and cars were inseparable in many communities in Brooklyn once the war was over and gas became plentiful again. This snapshot was taken in 1948 in front of Forman's Drug Store at Bay Parkway and Seventy-second Street.

around courts that shaded you from the summer sun or, in the winter, shielded your play from the biting winds. The fancier courts even had hedges and elaborate gardens (tended by the "super") and little iron fences that got painted, along with the fire escapes, every once in a while.

What practically everyone on every block had in common were the things that together gave the block its form: the sidewalk, divided into neat boxes, the curb, probably an irregular run of spalling bluestone, and the street pavement itself, if in fact it was paved and not just little crushed stones over a sticky-in-summer tar base. In the older sections, the roadbed was made of stone blocks that everyone incorrectly referred to as cobblestones, but in most parts of growing Brooklyn, streets were made of asphalt. In the less densely populated neighborhoods there was also a long, narrow earthen strip (that had no name) between the sidewalk edge and the curb. That was where one found trees and grass and where weeds multiplied and dogs were "walked," and where the many bare spots attracted games of immies—marbles—or, when you were old enough to have a pocket knife, "territories," in which a circle of dirt was sliced into national constituencies, just as Hitler and Mussolini and Tojo were doing at the time, out in the real

Ownership of a bicycle or tricycle offered childhood status, particularly if your cousin, bottom left, didn't have one. A Flatlands scene in 1950.

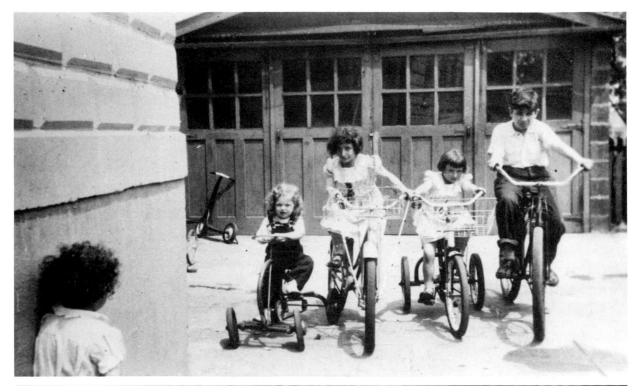

world. Later, in high school, the similarities of this pastime to the theorems of plane geometry were sure to escape you.

At the downhilliest corner—hard to believe there was one in the flats of Brooklyn—was the catchbasin, which everybody knew as the sewer (prounounced "*soo*-uh"), which was where the ball tended to wind up if your outfielder wore glasses. The little kids concealed Freudian fantasies of what would happen if they tried to climb down into the sewer to fish out the ball. But there was always a hefty teenager who'd volunteer, pry open the manhole cover with the end of the stickball bat (a broom handle) and descend carefully into the damp, smelly darkness. After what seemed an eternity he would pop out of the hole, the recovered ball held damply—and delicately—between thumb and forefinger, often to cheers from those assembled, before it was rolled dry in the gutter under a sneakered foot.

The street was not only the richest environment most Brooklyn kids could claim, but it was also one already calibrated to measure the physical attainments that came with increasing age. How many circuits of the block could be made on a tricycle or roller skates in a given time? How far could a fly ball be whacked? (A distance measured by counting manhole covers. Like catchbasins, they

In addition to stickball and touch football, Brooklyn's streets were also used for more formal games: A net and some equipment made paddle tennis possible along Bainbridge Street in Bedford-Stuyvesant in July of 1935.

Block after block of the borough's residential communities were lined with nineteenth-century brownstone (or brick) row houses often ornamented with bay windows and elaborate ironwork fences. These examples in Bed-Stuy indicate by their two and a half story height that they are somewhat far from dense downtown Brooklyn.

were also called "*soo*-uhs." A well-hit ball was either a one-sewer hit or a two-sewer—or, if you were eating your Wheaties, a three-sewer hit! *Splock!*)

The scored grooves of Brooklyn's sidewalks meant as much as the foul lines and nets of suburban tennis courts. Mastering their geometry didn't win loving cups or athletic letters, but proving one's ability at "hit-the-stick" (from an ice-cream pop), "box-ball," or "slam" was the way to develop a rep. Running an errand to the store could be paced by either stepping on the grooves or avoiding them—or, if you had the potential one day to be a candidate for Arista, every high school's honor society—devising some complex rhythm of one-on, two-off. They measured the lazy days of growing up in Brooklyn.

How was the street defined? Lots of Brooklyn's residences, large or small, single or multiple, rich or poor, displayed that great New York trademark, the stoop. Unlike the three spare, white steps of Baltimore's endless row houses, Brooklyn's almost always came accompanied by a hefty wall or balustrade that gave substance and sometimes even a sense of enclosure. To lots of kids who never had rooms of their own, that enclosure became the most easily available privacy they had. Some early coed exercises, like "doctor and nurse," were pursued in such semiprivate settings. It was where you could apply decalcomanias to the backs of your hands in peace. (Called decals today, we called them "cockamamies" then.) And when the stoop itself was not already occupied by grownups surveying the street life from their own informal amphitheaters, the steps made a terrific place to play "stoop ball," in which a hard-flung ball was bounced off the rounded nosing of a step and, one hoped, right past the hands of your opponent (a run), or into his hands after a bounce or two (a hit).

Cast-iron fire hydrants—"johnny pumps" to some—were what you hurdled, hands braced on their five-sided bronze pommels. Boys who missed rarely lived to tell the tale in a low voice. Telephone poles were what "johnny-on-the-pony" was played against, or what reworked peach baskets were nailed to for a game of one-on-one basketball played by two. Jacks and jumprope and double-dutch and skelly or potsy were played everywhere. For potsy—

Spurred on by heavy newspaper coverage, a crowd of twenty-five thousand descended upon Floyd Bennett Field on July 14, 1938, to greet thirty-two-year-old Howard Hughes and his three companions upon completion of their record-breaking round-the-world flight.

hopscotch to you?—skate keys did double duty, or house keys, which you were given if both your folks had to work. And with all the places your block offered to hide from friends, few days went by without a game of "hinegoseek" (a corruption from which the language may never recover) or the more sophisticated ringolevio.

The red-painted fire-alarm box and its tempting bronze handle, mounted high enough from the sidewalk to make short kids think twice, remained only an enticement for most. It was rumored that an unnecessary trip to a false alarm cost the fire department twenty-five dollars in gasoline, an inconceivable sum then, and that was the amount they made you pay if you were caught! But when the *clickety clack* spring-wound bell did go off, kids on the block scrambled quickly to the alarm box, arriving long before the engines did and affecting broad expressions of innocence, whispering, "Who did it? Who did it?" No one ever asked, "Where's the fire?"

Looking up at the sky brought all kinds of weird patterns to your eyes. Squeezing the lids hard brought even more. But looking up in this era revealed more than optical peculiarities and clouds. Flight had come to Brooklyn. Floyd Bennett Field had opened at the end of Flatbush Avenue in 1931. Every once in a while there'd be a plane—in the thirties, quite a special event. Some of them might even be trying for some kind of world's record. Wiley Post and Howard Hughes flew around the world from Floyd Bennett. Jacqueline Cochrane and Amelia Earhart advanced the cause of feminism with their flights from its runways. Flying a $900 second-hand crate, Douglas "Wrong Way" Corrigan chose Brooklyn as his point of departure to fly, as he told everyone, to California. He wound up in Ireland the next day. It was also the era of the dirigible. The U.S. Navy's *Akron* and *Shenandoah,* and the German zeppelin *Hindenburg*—all ill-fated—all made trips over New York. Awesome they were, overhead.

A treat was watching the skywriters, who flew single planes then, not a whole computerized formation. The plane itself flew so high it was hardly visible except when it rolled over and, for an instant, sent a piercing sliver of sunlight back to Brooklyn's sod. We especially longed for the airborne commercials of New York's super-salesman furrier, I. J. Fox. Whenever they appeared, you could be certain some acne-covered one among us would remember the routine: "Say it fast! Say, 'I. J. Fox's wife,' fast. Faster! Get it? 'I. J. Focks His Wife!' Ha, ha, ha!"

As evocative as the sky could be for some, the street back then

Horse-drawn wagons were a common sight along Brooklyn's thoroughfares well into the 1950s. Milk was delivered door-to-door by a number of dairies that refused to knuckle under to motorized conveyances. Rolling vegetable and fruit wagons came along the street straight to the housewife's kitchen. Some neighborhoods even had a traveling tin shop, captured by Berenice Abbott's lens in 1936.

Store rents were high enough in the 1930s that some marginal entrepreneurs were reduced to pushcart peddling along the curb of many a Brooklyn street, this one in Brownsville.

was clearly the more animated, more colorful place. More happened there than today. Local commerce, for example, was in greater evidence.

Near the freight sidings of the Long Island or South Brooklyn Rail Road, daily gatherings of pushcart peddlers, Old World style, made street markets of places like Brownsville's Belmont Avenue, or Borough Park's Thirteenth Avenue, or Moore Street in Williamsburg. There were fifty-eight such markets in the city in 1934–35, supporting almost fourteen thousand pushcart peddlers, until fastidious Mayor Fiorello LaGuardia decided that only indoor markets could produce the sanitary conditions that the New World required. (Belmont Avenue, which never got an indoor facility, persevered and prospered!) But more commonly, produce was hawked from individual pushcarts at subway stops all over Brooklyn, where people arriving home from work could be counted upon to buy at the low-overhead prices. Competition was rampant, and it was often price that made the sale. In those pre–Magic Marker days, "specials" would be written large with crudely conspicuous flourishes and serifs, in thick black crayon on giant-sized upside-down paper bags slipped over wood staves ripped from orange crates: "3 for 10¢," "2 lbs/25¢," "FRESH—5¢/lb." (Why would people who chose to make a living selling bananas and potatoes have such a natural knack for graphics?)

Back then, before the supermarkets (the first in this area didn't arrive until 1930—and in Queens, thank God), purveyors of food and other domestic needs made their way directly to the doorsteps

of less mobile, homebound housewives, rather than the other way around, thus reducing for many a homemaker the frequency of tiring journeys to the store.

Dawn often broke with the clip-clop of the milkman's horse making its rounds. The horse got to know the route and would lazily anticipate the next stop while the milkman moved from house to house. Bottles of milk (with a topping of unhomogenized cream) were ordered from Sheffield Farms, Borden's, Reid's Union Dairy, or some closer supplier by a note stuck into the empties the night before. Street sounds of horses' hooves contrasted later in the day with the soft squish of the Ward's Baking Company trucks delivering Tip Top bread and the Railway Express Agency's distinctive green delivery vans, which seemed to glide over the pavements, so silently did they run. Their wheels had solid rubber tires and the vans were powered electrically, like submarines running underwater, by ranks of wet-cell batteries stored in an underslung box that was so big it practically scraped the asphalt. And don't forget trucks that delivered laundry or freshly laundered diapers, or the dark-green-on-light-green delivery trucks of Krug's Bakery, with sloping fronts that sported the same profile as Dick Tracy's chin.

More to the point, however, housewives were saved countless shopping trips by stores-on-wheels that regularly rolled right down their block. Fruits and vegetables, baked goods, and that old standby, seltzer, were sold practically on one's doorstep if not in the kitchen itself. Fuller Brush men worked door-to-door, and so did Electrolux vacuum-cleaner salesmen. There were even Wearever aluminum parties that resembled today's for Tupperware. The Wearever folks would prepare a free meal in a neighbor's house and then make a pitch for sales.

"I cash clothes. I cash clothes." As the windows were opened to let in the gentle spring breezes, and window screens were liberated from winter hibernation, the familiar call of the neighborhood ragpicker would waft from the sidewalk and mix with the sounds of "Our Gal Sunday" or "Young Widder Brown" being played on nearby Motorolas or Stromberg-Carlsons. The season for spring cleaning would also mysteriously call forth the sounds of a junkman's cowbells. Recycling was even more a way of life then than it is now. Every able-bodied boy, for example, derived strength from wearing his dad's recycled felt fedora, its brim removed, its edges pinked and folded up like a sailor hat, sporting diamond-shaped holes for summer ventilation and bedecked with

The itinerant wet-plate street photographer was no Bachrach, but for many he was responsible for their first photograph. Invariably the camera was accompanied by what everyone identified as a Shetland pony. From the smiles in this snapshot, who cared?

The arrival of domestic refrigerators in the early thirties spurred fancy structures like this Rex Cole showroom at 6528 Fourth Avenue in Bay Ridge. Designed by the RCA Building's architect, Raymond Hood, it carried a larger-than-life replica of a GE refrigerator atop its roof.

election campaign buttons and school G.O. pins. That's where *Archie Comics'* Jughead got his.

Horse-and-wagon combinations, for junkmen and every other mobile merchant, were a common sight in the twenties and thirties, the gasoline shortages of World War II extending their usefulness well into the forties. After the war, a truck would substitute, but usually one that had seen better days. For once, the unrepaired potholes of the city's streets would perform a useful purpose: they would shake the junkman's wagon or truck, jangling his discordant cowbell carillon to announce his arrival. And periodically there would appear the scissors sharpener, the umbrella repairman, the organ-grinder, or the itinerant wet-plate photographer with a Shetland pony, ready to capture you with all the verisimilitude of the first gray-on-gray Polaroid pictures. Together, these street hawkers could populate a latter-day painting by Breughel, except none of us knew then who Breughel was.

To kids, the arrival of spring was marked not so much by the appearance of the robin, as our schoolteachers would have had it, but by jingling bells other than the junkman's, more sonorous ones this time, those of the mobile ice-cream vendors, of the "G'Jooma (Good Humor) man" on his adult-size tricycle, or the frozen-custard truck. (The words "soft ice cream" simply never caught on.) "Hey, let's get a Bungalow Bar!" would be heard, and the white and blue four-wheeled miniature bungalow with russet-shingled roof arrived to bring architectural variety to parts of Brooklyn that badly needed it, where houses, row after monotonous row of them, repeated their predictable fronts as far as the eye could see.

Ice was even better than ice cream. It was free—if you could get away with it, shards pilfered from the back of the absent iceman's truck. The refrigerator—everyone said "Frigidaire"—was making its way into more and more homes; the signs on the sides of new apartment buildings always assured you of a Kelvinator or a General Electric, the one with that funny cylindrical top (it held a hermetically sealed compressor, in case you're still wondering). But iceboxes were still pretty common then. And many of those who were saddled with those old-fashioned devices had a habit of storing perishables in cold chests under their kitchen windows in the winter months. One saved money that way. Where did the ice come from but a Rubel's ice truck? Slung over the burly iceman's strong shoulder and balanced precariously by ice tongs, a cake arrived every few days, and more often in the hot, humid summer. And there were always a few good words for the lady of the house, even flirtatious ones when called for. We couldn't wait till the ice truck was gone so we could taste our treasure. Mmmmn. Good. Cold. Funny, ice didn't have too much taste.

Iceboxes have disappeared, but ice cream is still sold this way on the streets of Brooklyn's neighborhoods, and so are frankfurters and Italian (now Puerto Rican) ices, both cupped and shaved. But what of the sweet potato man, pushing his silver-painted rolling oven? The corn-on-the-cob vendor? The jelly-apple merchant (thought by some suspicious mothers to be working in cahoots with the local dentist)? All gone.

Those neighborhood street people whose attire included a tin cup seemed also to open up a wider world to the kids. Invariably they were marginal souls who appeared—sometimes regularly, sometimes unpredictably—from out of nowhere, "nowhere" being a mysterious place that every one of us wanted one day to see. Some were colorfully dressed or had undecipherable accents or sported wild mustaches or had some kind of physical handicap that repelled as much as it attracted. No one knew who they were, and the give-and-take was sometimes filled with love and other times with harassment of a sort that only kids know how to sling and thick-skinned mendicants have learned to fend off.

Then there were the others. Pariahs of a different sort. What did we know? Interracial couples. The neighborhood handyman. His vehicle was an old baby carriage in which he transshipped heaps of old newspapers when he wasn't helping clean out some cellar of junk or move an old bedframe. Whole families who kept to themselves—"creature people," some called them.

Even those door-to-door vendors whose goods or services were compensated for on a more familiar, mercantile, this-for-that basis, could inadvertently, by their homey philosophy, expand the boundaries of the block and the expectations of its residents. One vendor's vocation required his taking a large box full of baked goods, cupcakes, pastries, and pies up apartment house elevators to announce, as he opened the door at every floor, "Doooooo-gan's! Doooooo-gan's!" Tired at the end of yet another day, he would pat a kid on the head and caution, "You go to college, ya hear? Otherwise, *you'll* become a Dugan's man . . . like me."

Coal and ice went the way of the horse and buggy during these years. One of many concrete coal bunkers in Brooklyn in those days, the Rubel Company's, off Atlantic Avenue in East New York, made a powerful impact on the flat horizon.

8

AW, MA, I DON'T WANNA GO

xcept for the mobility afforded by the postwar boom in automobiles, and the FHA's generosity to veterans and tract-house developers, it was a Brooklyn education that was responsible for dispersing its population so far and wide.

Although Brooklyn's schools were much criticized in those days they *did* teach. On every level.

Brooklyn had an awful lot of P.S.'s and J.H.S.'s, with numbers reaching into the 300s. Some, it seems, were so impoverished that they carried *only* a number. Most, however, carried a name as well, perhaps a hero from history or an obscure local son— rarely a daughter, then—dredged up on sleepless nights by ambitious assistant superintendents of schools: good old Almon G. Merwin, P.S. 74. Or Algernon S. Higgins, P.S. 111. And don't forget Silas B. Dutcher, P.S. 124.

Some Catholic schools could be distinguished from one another by the girls' uniforms and, of course, by the quality of the teaching, mostly done by plain-faced nuns or brothers whose strict discipline subdued even the most recalcitrant. They integrated themselves into the American system by having their older students sell "chances" in lotteries designed to fund various church causes. Other parochial schools, such as the yeshivas in the Jewish neighborhoods, had a much harder time weaving their archaic traditions into the values of twentieth-century life, which everywhere enveloped their pupils. After-school *talmud torahs* taught bar mitzvah lessons; Sholem Aleichem schools taught Yiddish secular culture.

There were ritzy schools, too: Packer Collegiate Institute, on

Going to school was fine for some kids but playing truant at the local movie house, maybe the Lakeland under the BMT elevated on Brighton Beach Avenue, was even better. Roller-skating there in your new knickers was the best.

Except for the cars—and the open space along the curb—it's hard to tell anything has changed along Joralemon Street in Brooklyn Heights since this photograph of Packer Collegiate Institute was taken in the early thirties.

Joralemon Street in Brooklyn Heights, for example; and Poly Prep, out behind Fort Hamilton. James Agee found Poly's students of the 1940s to be among those "first-flight gentiles [streaming] . . . into Williams and Princeton, the second flight into Colgate or Cornell. . . ." He also noted how much other groups also valued higher education: ". . . the Jews whose whole families are breaking their hearts for it from Boys High into Brooklyn College and Brooklyn Law, and the luckiest of them into Harvard. . . ."

If it wasn't the Ivy League or NYU or LIU or St. John's that beckoned, then perhaps it was Brooklyn College for you, at least after 1930. Brooklyn College between 1908 and 1921 was the name of a small Roman Catholic college allied with Brooklyn Prep, located on Nostrand Avenue near Carroll Street in Crown Heights. By 1930, however, its name had been assumed by the Brooklyn College we know today, which became the city's third public college, joining famed City and Hunter, but the first in the municipal system to be coeducational. At first, classes were taught only in downtown Brooklyn, an outgrowth of courses given in the twenties as part of CCNY's extension program.

In 1935, ground was finally broken for Brooklyn College's own campus in Flatbush, on a forty-three-acre former golf course, the Wood-Harmon tract, where the IRT Nostrand Avenue trains ended their run. On October 28, 1936, President Franklin Delano Roosevelt arrived at the site to help lay the cornerstone for the gym. It was the New Deal's Federal Emergency Public Works

Administration, whose grants and loans were designed to put people back to work during the Great Depression, that spurred campus construction. Election Day was only a few days away. Roosevelt wanted a second term, and Brooklyn was then—as now—the home of a lot of registered Democrats.

In the years since the dedication of the campus, such well-known figures as Oscar Handlin, Alfred Drake, Sam Levenson, the Marxist critic Eugene Genovese, and even Bernie Cornfeld, the stock promoter, have spent time in Boylan Hall and the other red brick, white-trimmed, out-of-scale, neo-Georgian buildings that tried to look like Harvard on the barrenness of their Flatbush site. Lost in their Ivy League fantasies, few of the students realized that it really *didn't* look like Harvard Yard.

The same year Brooklyn College opened its new campus, the city paid $950,000 for the tax-delinquent Elks Club hotel in downtown Brooklyn, which society architects McKim, Mead & White had designed in the palmier days of the twenties. With the rapid expansion of the city's school population in the post–World War I years, there simply wasn't enough room for the growing numbers of educational administrators in the handsome but cramped structure at Manhattan's 500 Park Avenue. Thus began the checkered career of 110 Livingston Street as the central headquarters of the New York City Board of Education. "*Bored* of Education," sharp kids quipped. It wasn't long before rumors began to fly that some of the school system's most intractable and embarrassing teachers had been reassigned as tenured administrative exiles on the upper floors at Livingston and Boerum. (William Boylan, first president of Brooklyn College, was recruited from a position at the Board of

Tax exemption for those who got in before the deadline and the image of a brand new school awaiting the influx of newcomers' children were among the attractions for attending this auction.

Ed, where he supervised public-school site selection and construction; he was also Mayor Walker's good friend and onetime teacher.)

As the builders of the twenties began to scan Brooklyn's outlying emptiness for development sites, they saw only vast expanses of vacant lots and undeveloped meadows and swamps, lacking even the most rudimentary evidence of the urban. Soon, sewers, streets, sidewalks, utility poles, and, of course, freshly built schools began to proliferate, the schools looming over the new houses, most of which were only one or two stories high.

It was those taller schools, some with blank end walls evidently meant for extension as the vacant lots filled, that started to punctuate the otherwise flat, largely treeless plains of outer Brooklyn. Their silhouettes began to give a uniformity of character to the landscapes of that area, creating a scene, incidentally, that in some parts of Brooklyn looks curiously the same today.

Entering the heavy doors of the schools, you were engulfed by an aroma like that of a freshly opened can of Campbell's tomato soup. The newer schools, in contrast, reflected shorter histories and newer maintenance techniques: they reeked of disinfectants so strong that they suggested the custodian was exploring new directions for a cancer cure.

The school day, at least in the public schools, had a chaotic character, due mainly to frequent interruptions, first for the collection of money—in one's early years it was for milk and cookies,

When the Brooklyn Childrens Museum was still housed in two antique mansions in Brower Park, a typical weekend outing might have included butterfly hunting. Here, boys and girls wait for the trip to start.

the serving of which, at recess, was in itself another interruption. In the proper season came the sale of seeds (in plain brown wrappers from Brooklyn's own Botanic Garden) and things like amaryllis bulbs. Who knew the bulbs would look like overgrown onions? What a surprise when they finally arrived! "Don't forget, children. Put your bulbs in the darkest part of your cellar!" Those without cellars—most of us—had to negotiate a spot in an already over-crowded closet.

Then came the appeals from the Red Cross, the March of Dimes, War Savings Stamps. Many schools allowed the borough's banks to encourage "student thrift accounts" to start the savings habit young, and perhaps thus also to ensure a good supply of tomorrow's customers. Questions came to mind as one grew older. Did the inordinately large number of money collections have underlying motives? Were they a subtle way of institutionalizing capitalism? Did the teachers surreptitiously divide the milk and crackers left over from the inevitable absences? And speaking of absences, if it wasn't the grippe, flu, chicken pox, mumps, measles (regular and German), scarlet fever, rheumatic fever, tummyache—you name it—it was the common cold. ("Did you bring a note from your mother?") In some neighborhoods, fear of epidemics would fill the classrooms with the aroma of garlic or camphor balls, worn in carefully stitched little cloth sacks suspended from the necks of boys and girls with fearful mothers versed in superstition and skilled at sewing.

Every year, school children in all the boroughs eagerly awaited packets of seeds they had ordered from the Brooklyn Botanic Garden. Here a squad of young volunteers stands at the ready on the steps of the garden's administration building with seed orders clutched to their chests, about to fan out on delivery assignments to nearby schools.

Then there were the larger interruptions. The unpredictable—but regular—*clang, clang, clang, clang* of the fire-drill gong ("Size places, everyone!"). The IQ tests. The reading exams. ("What d'ya get, what d'ya get?") Once or twice a year came Health Day, when the unshampooed found out that red horseshoes on the scalp meant ringworm, and the squinters all fell prey to the eye chart at twenty paces. Soon eyeglasses would appear in the classroom, greeted by jeers of "Four eyes, four eyes!"

Despite what some believed were clear constitutional warnings to the contrary, city public schools offered "released time" to those students whose parents thought they needed a dose of religious instruction in the middle of the school week. (Did parochial schools offer comparable midweek relief from spiritual studies?)

Anyone bringing a note from home could take the assigned time off—was it Tuesday or Wednesday?—to attend class in a local church or synagogue. From the point of view of Catholic-school kids, this was a drag: they had to vacate their classrooms to allow the "visitors" to learn catechism every week. They would sullenly march to the auditorium, where, over and over, they saw the same devotional films: *The Bells of Saint Mary's, The Lou Gehrig Story, The Song of Bernadette.* And those who were left behind in the public schools, in addition to assuming the risk of being labeled whatever kids called those who challenged the very existence of G-d, wound up spending lazy afternoons when nothing significant could be taught. Girls sewed, boys built model airplanes. Or you could do what the teacher called "quiet reading" (as opposed to raucous reading, I guess).

Most dances were sponsored by the school, church, or social club, but sometimes an important event would bring a family together and everyone would get a chance for a spin on the dance floor. The little girls are wondering what this dance is called.

It may not have been quite the equivalent of the Katharine Gibbs School, but Brooklyn's Girls' Commercial High School, on Classon Avenue between Union and President streets, trained many a Brooklyn damsel to be a competent secretary in the years before word processors became the vogue in the business offices of the city.

Some students, like Alfred Kazin, measured the school term by the week: "All week long I lived for the blessed gong at three o'clock on Friday afternoon." But the most popular day of all, by general acclamation, was the last of the school year. Inevitably the humidity was pushing one hundred percent, the June sun would be broiling, and kids could be heard chanting, "No more lessons, no more books, no more teachers' dirty looks." After an interminable number of these annual punctuations, childhood was over and the start of the school year on the Monday after Labor Day brought either junior high or—*ta-ta-ta-taaa!*—the *real thing:* high school, one's graduation into the almost-adult world, at least then.

While elementary schools tended, because of their small size, to intensify neighborhood cohesiveness, bringing together as they did mostly children of the same age from the same area, junior-high schools and high schools were larger and drew their students from many different communities. Where residential densities were low, as in outer Brooklyn, trips to school for older students could mean a daily trolley or bus or subway ride. The mornings weren't so bad, with early birds and late arrivals spreading the load on the transit system. But at the three o'clock bell, it was bedlam when the whole school population poured down the stairways and through the doors, with almost everyone wanting to scramble aboard a conveyance to get home fast. What a crush!

Junior-high and high schools offered up such new treats as home room and shifting classes for every subject. With teachers seeing five sets of faces a day, a curious system evolved that used "Delaney cards"—little slips that teachers arranged in albums to duplicate the desk layout of each assigned class. How handy they were to identify culprits by name, check attendance, and note lateness! And every teacher had some kind of code about grades for homework assignments, test papers, and brilliant comments in class. They all learned to write tiny.

Rushing "up the down staircase" became a way of life—and only later the title of a popular book. Lunch rooms in the larger high schools were an education in themselves. Borrowing a fork or spoon required a special octagonal tag for which you paid a deposit at the start of the term, the tag returnable only upon return of the implement. During almost every lunch hour, amid interminable and inane public-address-system announcements, came, "Whoever lost a sterling silver pen and can identify it, please form a line at the cafeteria office!"

Those high school days also meant dating, when, for a lot of Brooklyn adolescents, Saturday night could be the loneliest night of the week. Depending on sex appeal and personality ("looks don't count, Doris—it's personality"), adventurousness, upbringing, family traditions, and the level of your own neurosis, you either went out or you didn't.

Dances were popular and there were plenty to choose from. Why else did they build high school gymnasiums?

Mixers and weekend dances were the currency of every Brooklyn institution catering to the teenage or young adult set. Scenes such as this could be found at high schools, community centers, or at any of Brooklyn's public or private colleges. This scene is at Pratt Institute in the 1940s.

Girls were placed on the earth to teach boys how to dance (some of both genders believed) and that's how many in Brooklyn learned, at least those who didn't come from a background where you were expected to take classes in social dancing. The two step. The fox trot. The Lindy. Jitter-bugging. Bobby sox. Big bands. *The One O'Clock Jump.* One-button-lounge, pegged pants, zoot suit. Frank Sinatra. Crooning. Swooning.

To try to keep ethnic, religious, and racial continuity intact, organizations representing those critical differentiations among Brooklyn's residents sponsored their own dances. The former Knights of Columbus hall on Prospect Park West and Union Street—now the Madonna Residence—was just one of many such places in Brooklyn for Saturday night socializing. The intent there was to bring Roman Catholic boys and girls together. But rumor had it that lots of Jewish girls came to mingle; they just didn't bother to tell their folks about it. Neither did many of the others.

Dances were organized as fund-raisers, too. A private dance hall like the Prospect Palace, still standing on Prospect Avenue, could be rented by neighborhood groups seeking to raise money. Capable of attracting crowds of as many as five hundred at a shot, sponsors such as local SACs—social and athletic clubs, groups whose members were entitled to wear those sateen jackets with their names stitched on the front—could raise quite a sum in just one night, even at a dollar a throw, if they could only unload enough tickets. There were lots of gangs and lots of rivalry. Sometimes dances themselves turned into brawls, blood baths even. The melees most times started with an argument over a girl. One thing led to another, and then, POW! Fists began to fly and all hell broke loose.

As the years passed and graduation approached, dates in ice cream parlors and going to the movies became kind of tame. For the older set there were the clubs on "the strip," Flatbush Avenue below Prospect Park: the Patio, the Parakeet Club, the Circus Lounge. Those were places where you went if you really wanted to bounce.

Even though time passed slowly, for many couples "going out" became serious—like "going steady." The common appellation used by parents, if not necessarily by teenagers, was "keepin' company." Some of those who went too far too soon wound up going as far as Maryland . . . for a shotgun wedding; Maryland didn't require a waiting period prior to issuing a marriage license. Sure, it wasn't a church wedding or anything like that, but lots of

Erasmus Hall High School, on Flatbush Avenue below Church, presented an imposing presence on the busy thoroughfare. Through the Tudor style archway the curious will find the original building of Erasmus Hall Academy, dating from 1786.

people in Brooklyn didn't go to church as much as they went to the cemetery.

Not all bopping around by boys was done in the company of girls. Even before reaching legal drinking age some were venturing into bars and hanging out in pool halls. At first you'd run errands for the older fellas bent over the green baize tables: get a pack of cigarettes or bring back a container of beer. Sometimes the owner would let you sweep up. Tips, you'd do it for tips. Money wasn't easy to come by. Lots of families didn't know from allowances. But they knew about curfews: ten o'clock and you had to be home.

If you did have some money to spare, picked up from tips or shining shoes, or something, you could go to the Monday night amateur hour at the Fox—where they yanked you off the stage with a hook if the audience got too raucous or started to boo. And there were the boxing matches, the fights, at the arena on Eastern Parkway Extension, or in the outdoor amphitheater in Coney Island where you could smell low tide in the nearby creek. During the war, you didn't even need money to see a ballgame at Ebbets Field: a piece of scrap iron or a bundle of newspapers would get you a seat in left field.

What with girls and needing to make money and all the distractions of sporting events and nights out with the boys it was not unheard of, even then, to drop out of high school. Even those who stayed didn't always cherish the experience.

To Matthew Josephson, author of *The Robber Barons,* his Brooklyn high school was "a famous grind factory." But others thought better of theirs, and opinions as to which of Brooklyn's many high schools was the best are as many as those asked. In those days, many thought Erasmus Hall was the intellectual peak. Its castellated structure dated from the turn of this century, but its heritage was Brooklyn's equivalent of Plymouth Rock. To this day, framed within Erasmus Hall's green courtyard, stands the small 1786 wood-clapboard building of Erasmus Hall Academy, founded by the venerable Dutch Reformed Church (across Flatbush Avenue from the school) and originally funded by gifts from the likes of Alexander Hamilton and Aaron Burr. Among its many distinguished graduates are inventor Elmer Sperry, Hollywood actresses Aline McMahon and Barbra Streisand, chess champ Bobby Fischer, and Ruby Stevens, who later achieved fame using the name Barbara Stanwyck.

A dozen years earlier, along tree-shaded Marcy Avenue, in what is today called Bedford-Stuyvesant, was built an even more richly conceived architectural gem, Boys High School. Bertram D. Wolfe, authority on Russian and Hispanic culture, taught there. Both Isaac Asimov and Norman Mailer studied there. Radio personalities Gabriel Heatter and Clifton Fadiman (of "Information Please"), as well as "Meet the Press"'s Lawrence Spivak, learned

The spectacular Boys High School building, on Marcy and Putnam avenues, no longer houses the school. Together with companion Girls High, whose original structure stands nearby at 475 Nostrand Avenue, the two were mated into a low-rise Boys and Girls High built in the 1970s along Fulton Street.

public speaking there. Arnold Moss and Alan King graduated from Boys High to appear on the stage, and other alumni include philosopher Sidney Hook, architect Morris Lapidus, Levvittown builder William J. Levitt, and Rabbi Alfred Gottschalk, a leader of American Reform Judaism. And there would be no Ellery Queen mysteries if Manfred B. Lee, a Boys High boy, and Frederic Dannay, hadn't collaborated.

Girls High's red-painted Gothic Revival building turned out actress Florence Eldridge, singer Lena Horne, and Bedford-Stuyvesant's member of the House of Representatives, Shirley Chisholm (née St. Hill), class of '42. Prospect Heights High School, another all-girls institution, was Susan Hayward's alma mater.

In Brooklyn's north, the two high schools were Eastern District and Bushwick. Joseph Hirshhorn (who endowed Washington's Hirshhorn Museum) attended both but graduated from neither. Alumni of Eastern District include Henry Miller, author of all those smarmy novels we used to smuggle into class; comedy star Mel Brooks, then known as Melvyn Kaminsky, who lived at 111 Lee Avenue; the Boston Celtics' basketball personality Arnold "Red" Auerbach ('34); and composer-singer Barry Manilow, who entered in '57. Bushwick's pride includes Chock Full O' Nuts entrepreneur and philanthropist Charles Black and Hollywood film producer Irving Thalberg, on whom Budd Schulberg's *What Makes Sammy Run* is reputed to have been based.

Manual Training's name struck fear in the hearts of athletes

Bay Ridge High School, the all-girls school at Fourth Avenue and Senator Street, gleams in this official portrait taken when it was new in 1913.

Brooklyn Technical School, Brooklyn, N. Y.

MANUAL TRAINING HIGH SCHOOL, SEVENTH AVENUE AND FIFTH STREET, BROOKLYN, N. Y.

The former Manual Training—now John Jay—High School, and the original Brooklyn Tech, which initially occupied a former factory building at 49 Flatbush Avenue Extension near the Manhattan Bridge, were important enough in their communities to merit recognition on penny postcards.

throughout the borough. A tough school with tough players. Nevertheless, Manual graduated deep-voiced radio and television narrator Alexander Scourby; author Quentin Reynolds; actress Thelma Ritter; comedian Henny Youngman; baseball player Joe Pepitone; and Nobel laureate Dr. Isidor Isaac Rabi.

Out in eastern Brooklyn, in the Brownsville, East New York, and Canarsie sections, the schools were Jefferson and Lane. David Daniel Kominski, a Thomas Jefferson student with a twinkle in his eye, later changed his name to Danny Kaye. Shelley Winters, though born in St. Louis, relocated to Brooklyn and became editor of the Jefferson newspaper. Franklin K. Lane numbered among its students Alfred Kazin ('31), author of *A Walker in the City* and *New York Jew;* Anne Jackson ('43); Earl Hyman ('43); William "Red" Holzman ('38), New York Knicks coach and general manager; and the president of the Ford Foundation, Franklin A. Thomas ('52).

The borough's all-city high school, Brooklyn Tech, accepted

only those who passed an entrance exam. Numbered among its graduates are Nobel Prize winners Dr. George Wald and Dr. Arno Penzias; Dr. Irwin Shapiro, director of the Harvard-Smithsonian Center for Astrophysics; and Lt. Col. Karol Bobko, one of America's astronauts. It has its share of municipal officials—Thomas F. Galvin, president of the Jacob K. Javits Convention Center; Commissioner of Sanitation Norman Steisel; Traffic Commissioner Samuel I. Schwartz; and Vice Chairman of the Landmarks Preservation Commission, Elliot Willensky. Tech also educated people prominent outside the technical world: Harvey Lichtenstein, president of the Brooklyn Academy of Music (and a former modern dancer himself); Gordon Davidson, artistic director of the Mark Taper Forum in Los Angeles; Marshall Brickman, noted screenwriter and Woody Allen collaborator. In Brooklyn's southern tier, the area that exploded with new populations after 1920, we find the most remarkable array of talent. At Abraham Lincoln: authors Joseph Heller and Arthur Miller; critic Ken Auletta; Nobel Prize winners Dr. Arthur Kornberg and Dr. Arthur Berg; Kings County District Attorney Elizabeth Holtzman; actor Louis Gossett, Jr.; composer Neil Sedaka; baseball star Lee Mazzilli; graphic designer Seymour Chwast. At James Madison: opera star Elaine Malbin and composer-singer Carole King; playwright Garson Kanin; author and educator Barry Commoner; journalists Sylvia Porter and Jane Brody; sports announcer Marty Glickman; baseball star Cal Abrams; sports promoter David "Sonny" Werblin; William M. Gaines, MAD magazine's founder. At Midwood: author Erich Segal; author, actor, director, clarinetist Woody Allen; actress Didi Conn; composer John Corigliano; Anthony Gliedman, New York City Commissioner of Housing Preservation and Development; and Congressman Stephen Solarz, who was elected Mayor of Midwood—as the head of its student body is called—in '57–'58. At New Utrecht: singers Richard Tucker, Robert Merrill, and

Every high school had a general organization—G. O. for short—and a G. O. store, where incidentals like notebooks and gym shorts and school buttons and banners were sold. At Tech the homeroom teacher was called a prefect. Very pretentious.

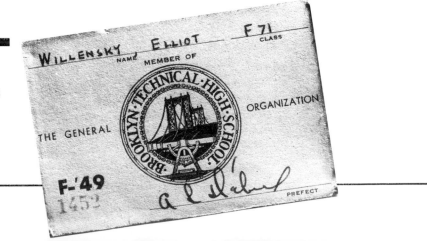

Midwood High School was built just up Bedford Avenue, across from the Brooklyn College campus, just before the onset of World War II.

Doretta Morrow; playwright Abe Burrows; comedians Buddy Hackett, Phil Silvers, Phil Foster, Jack Carter, and Arnold Stang; and "Candid Camera"'s Allen Funt. At Samuel J. Tilden: authors Irving Shulman (*The Amboy Dukes*) and Gerald Green (*The Last Angry Man*); singers Abbe Lane and Helen Forrest; TV columnist Earl Ubell; labor leader Victor Gotbaum; attorney Leonard Garment; Judges Milton Mollen and Leonard Yoswein; baseball stars Willie Randolph and Sid Gordon. At Lafayette: former Dodger pitcher Sandy Koufax; Larry King, the late-night radio personality; fashion designer Ron Chereskin; designer/artist Peter Max; and Maurice Sendak, whose children's books are memorable both for his stories and illustrations.

One of the thousands of men and women who made their way through Brooklyn's schools and later achieved fame was author Irwin Shaw. He summed up his Brooklyn experiences in a special way. Long after he had graduated he recalled his alma mater, Brooklyn College, as "a wonderful school. . . . It was free and it taught me all I needed to know to get out of Brooklyn."

9
A PLACE OF COAL SMOKE AND ASHES

T here was no OPEC to manipulate oil prices. Natural gas didn't exist, either, except as a waste product in the search for crude. Petroleum was what gasoline, benzene, kerosene, and Vaseline were made of. For most of us in Brooklyn, houses were heated by coal: bituminous (made illegal somewhere along the way), anthracite, or something the ads called "Blue Coal."

In the winter the skies over Brooklyn were filled with dark smoke rising from the chimneys of apartment houses. To many it was a sign that "there was steam," which meant that by the time you got home, your apartment might no longer have that damp chill about it. ("Steam," the medium of heat transfer in most Brooklyn residences, in the minds of some European immigrants, took on the meaning of "heat." To this day, when an automobile heater is turned on, some exclaim, "Oh, feel, there's steam!")

In the poorer neighborhoods, in sections such as Gowanus or Williamsburg or Red Hook, there were still "belly stoves," the pot bellies whose exuberant shapes seemed to fill a room with warmth even when there wasn't enough coal to keep it fired. Poor families were often large families, too, and the younger boys were sent out to follow the coal trucks to bring back chunks that the irregular street pavement caused the brimful trucks to offload as they made their way to more middle-class sections of the borough.

The same fuel that fired winter's furnaces also fired summer's hot-water tanks, filling the sky with wispier black streaks. The smell of coal smoke would be in the air. And the raspy sound of

Alongside the Gowanus Canal the Brooklyn Union Gas Company maintained a number of spidery telescoping gas tanks, each holding an enormous volume of water gas for Brooklyn's household and industrial uses.

the super's coal shovel scraping the cellar's concrete floor could be discerned in the early quiet (along with sea gulls' calls) as soft light filled the sky and it was hazily evident that it was morning again.

Coal not only made a dependable fuel, but was also useful for making graffiti, though not as good as broken plaster. (*No one bought chalk in the candy store if a demolition job was under way on the block.*) Coal was also what gave a snowman his eyes, nose, and mouth. But somehow snowstorms and available pieces of coal rarely came together when needed.

As coal was the fuel for heating, gas was the fuel for cooking. Wood had become old-fashioned and electricity was newfangled, and anyway, no one's wiring was thick enough to accommodate the amount needed for heating. As soon as gas became a common household commodity, it began to attract the fantasies of those bent upon taking their lives. Newspapers were full of such events, particularly during the Depression. Harried mothers threatened to "take the gas pipe," producing nightmares among their children if not necessarily extracting good behavior.

In those days, before technology made it possible to collect natural gas economically and pump it through transcontinental pipelines, cooking gas was made locally by Brooklyn's utility companies. In other places, such as The Bronx, it was a byproduct of the manufacture of coke, produced by the cooking of coal. Making

When coal was the preferred fuel for just about everything except the new cars, giant coal bunkers of timber or concrete were built all over Brooklyn. This one, calling itself "World's Largest Retail Coal Yard," stood at the edge of Newtown Creek.

coke was a particularly colorful process in winter when it produced billows of pure white water vapor as the glowing prisms of coke were rammed from the enormous ovens and quenched with a colossal bath of water. Of course, all this went on behind the high walls of the gas house, so that only the white plumes of vapor, rising high in the chilly sky, were witnessed by the locals. In Brooklyn a method called the "carbureted water-gas process" was used. It was less colorful but more fetid. What a stink! You could always tell you were near the gasworks even when blindfolded. No one wanted to live near them, and those who did had a constant reminder of their poverty in the gasworks' distinctive mark, the tanks. Silhouetted in the sky, enveloped by enormous, lacy cylindrical networks of iron and steel, they actually were quite beautiful. Many were located along Brooklyn's waterways, where the raw materials could be delivered cheaply by barge: the Gowanus, Newtown or Coney Island Creek (which had a different kind of gas tank, the taller, more modern stationary type), and in other places, like the waterfront at Fifty-fifth Street, where they can still be found. As the supply and demand changed, the telescoping gas tanks rose and fell imperceptibly along upright tracks fastened to their delicate cages. It was said that on Thanksgiving or Christmas—when, of course, almost every oven in Brooklyn was in action and the demand for cooking gas was enormous—the tops of the tanks dropped almost to ground level.

Atlantic Avenue is no longer the home of Ex-Lax, the chocolated laxative, though the factory buildings are still in service as converted lofts for residential living. The clapboard furniture store is at the northwest corner of Nevins Street.

COAL POCKETS OF THE SCRANTON & LEHIGH COAL CO. BROOKLYN, N.Y.

OUR AIM BEST COAL BEST SERVICE PLEASED CUSTOMERS SCRANTON & LEHIGH COAL CO. THOMAS V. PATTERSON GENERAL MANAGER

NORTH 9TH STREET COAL POCKET.

NEWTOWN COAL POCKET.

WALLABOUT COAL POCKET.

GOWANUS COAL POCKET.

As sure as there was coal in those years in Brooklyn, there were also ashes, and the container that conveyed them from cellar and boiler room to refuse truck was the ash can. Ash cans were cousins to today's garbage cans. They achieved a certain éclat for having an American school of painting named after them. Ash cans were substantial, made of corrugated sheets of galvanized iron, riveted together and not vacuum-formed or injection-molded of polypropelene, or polyvinyl chloride, or some other esoteric petroleum derivative. Ash cans were meant to do a heavy job, and took a considerable beating. Dropped (as they usually were) from the top of the garbage truck where they were emptied, they crashed with a resounding clatter.

These containers carried a noble name, for theirs was a noble task: carrying ashes. The mysterious residue of coal was a wondrous thing, picturesque in and of itself, and capable of many reuses. Unlike today's garbage, filled as it is with the nonbiodegradable products of a grotesquely overdeveloped packaging industry, ashes had a poetic constancy about them. Virtually weightless, the soft gray pumice contained sharp-edged, convoluted lumps of iridescent ochre and orange and blue-black that sometimes resembled the fragments of meteorites displayed at the Hayden Planetarium. These ashes had withstood infernos in the cellars of Brooklyn; in a place lacking a volcano, ashes were Brooklyn's lava.

Ashes also had subsidiary uses that enriched the city's character. How symbiotic that the winter season, when coal was most in use and when ash cans brimmed with their abrasive contents, was also the season when Brooklyn's streets would ice up. Weary sanitation men were only too glad when the cans were emptied onto glazed streets and sidewalks in order to improve traction, turning Brooklyn a drab gray in the process. When snow and cold weather were prolonged, the streets would cake up as though with some sort of proto-concrete. In one bad year in the thirties, the city had to use penumatic drills to break up the accumulation.

In the years of coal, ashes were the city's number-one solid waste. Before the reforms of the LaGuardia administration, the city's Department of Sanitation was an embarrassment. Everything about it was khaki-colored (to camouflage the inefficiencies, no doubt) except the hats worn by its members when posing for publicity shots—white with black visors and shaped like those of the police. The most sophisticated of the Department's activities was stenciling a motto on its curbside public trash receptacles:

BY LAW
ABIDE
PUT
TRASH
INSIDE
D.S.

To empty ash cans in those days, two muscular sidewalk men had to hoist each can some six feet into the air to be tipped into the hoppers of the city's primitive, open-to-the-sky, khaki-colored sanitation trucks. Booted and knee-deep in teabags and orange peels, and inured to the buzzing, iridescent bluebottle flies, the sanit man in the truck would then upturn the ash can, empty it, and drop it over the side, back onto the pavement—crash! It was a scene repeated tour after tour, day after day, and one that quickly caught the eye of the 1930s reform mayor. It wasn't long before "the Little Flower" introduced sleek, light gray, totally covered trucks that required only a forty-inch lift to empty the cans onto the mechanical conveyors that protruded from their back ends. The future had come to Brooklyn. Years had to pass before the machinery of the modern trucks began to grind and groan as city maintenance fell behind, until it was *their* sounds that could be discerned in the early quiet (along with sea gulls' calls) as soft light filled the sky and it was hazily evident that it was morning again.

These LaGuardia administration drawings barely convey a proper appreciation of the environmental change that occurred when the old garbage trucks were replaced by the Sanitation Department with mechanical loaders.

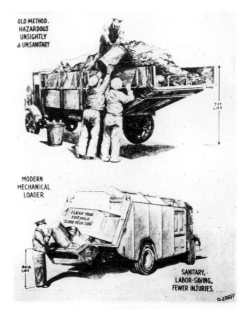

10

WALK US
TO THE STORE

The postwar flight to suburbia was well along before retailers, marketing pundits, and sociological investigators came to realize that shopping was not only a day-in-day-out part of life for some, but also an enjoyable way of passing time and an easy source of entertainment.

When a mother announced "Poppa needs a suit, I need a dress, and you, you need shoes," it was time to take a trip to the neighborhood's big-time shopping street. It was a real event, one that could last all day. In Flatbush, it was Flatbush Avenue, which went on for miles. In Brownsville, it was Pitkin Avenue. Others were identified by overhead elevateds: Broadway, which acted like a zipper joining Williamsburg and Bed-Stuy, 86th Street in Bensonhurst, Fulton Street in downtown Brooklyn, Fifth Avenue stretching between South Brooklyn and Sunset Park. The narrow part of Kings Highway, which was—and still is—such a homey, friendly, and crowded place to shop, became such a regional mecca that the residential neighborhood around it assumed the same name.

Even the trip to shop was a shopping experience. Subway stations had newsstands, but even better, practically every iron pillar had penny vending machines. The tall, baked-enamel ones were Wrigley's domain. After you deposited your coin in the right slot, you twisted an S-shaped dial: Spearmint, Doublemint, Juicy Fruit, P.K. (P.K.? What ever happened to those two fat white lozenges of gum in the yellow, red, and green packet?) The smaller machines were gleaming, chromium-plated, glass-fronted devices dispensing Hershey's line; they required pulling the right lever for

In the thirties, lucky charms in the form of shiny, brass-plated tokens resembling horseshoes accompanied the purchase of Kali-Stenik children's shoes. Later they were silver in color and had a bright shiny new penny in the center.

Milk Chocolate, same with Almonds, and Bittersweet, which your mother thought was better for you because it didn't taste as sweet. The penny Hersheys all had that funny shape, like gold ingots. And, of course, every once in a while you'd come upon a pillar with a glass globe half-filled with peanuts, which always left your little hands salty and greasy. When technology came to the subway after the war, automatic soda machines appeared; all too often the liquid spurted but the cup wasn't there. It was an early sign that Russia might beat us with Sputnik.

Except for the modernistic Sears Roebuck that opened in Flatbush in 1932, and the small Macy's branch that opened close by after the war, Brooklyn's department stores were confined to Fulton Street, downtown. The remaining shopping hubs had specialty stores, both independent retailers and branches of chains. The chains had names we all remember, some of which still exist. There were shoe stores like Thom McAn and Regal for men, and A.S. Beck, Miles, and Red Cross for women. In addition there were also the buzzword brands: Enna Jettick, Pedi-Forme, Treadeasy, and Propr-Wauk, not to mention Kali-Sten-Iks, and Dr. Posner's Scientific Shoes, made especially for the younger set. Brooklyn must have suffered from a collective foot fetish. Remember looking at a fluoroscope X-ray of your feet through the big brown box that resembled your family's floor-model Philco? Do you ever wonder whether tumors will eventually show up on your toes, your eyelids, or your salesman?

Women's fashions were represented by Lerners, Rainbow Shops, or Lane Bryant's, with Fisher Brothers (now in Cedarhurst) at 1621 Pitkin Avenue. Men's and boys' suits and coats were available through Crawford, Howard, or Ripley, or from shirt shops that gained respectability from featuring the larger name brands—Arrow, Van Heusen, Manhattan. Simon Ackerman not only sold men's suits and coats, but made them in a factory at 1213 East New York Avenue. And sporting goods were a big thing then, too. Remember the big neon signs reading VIM, or DAVEGA?

The big purchases were furniture and jewelry, and in those days before plastic money—before credit cards—shopping meant credit furniture stores and jewelry chains and putting yourself in hock for what seemed forever: don't confuse the furniture of Michael Brothers with J. Michael's, Inc., or Michaels & Company. Competition was keen. (Which of the Michaels had the streamlined Art Moderne–style storefronts so fashionable in the late thirties?) As for jewelry chains, there were Busch's Kredit Jewelers and

Finlay Straus, among others; somehow Boschwitz's, an independent jeweler of a higher cut, on Fifth Avenue in Bay Ridge, is still family-owned today. Is there hope?

Sometimes a retail store, like Max Fortunoff's, under the New Lots line el at 561 Livonia Avenue, was such a magnet in itself that it needed no shopping strip to prosper. Loehmann's also was such a shop. Beginning in 1922, it occupied a two-story structure at 1476 Bedford Avenue (at Sterling Place), whose Chinese gold-leaf dragons still survive—now embellishing a black storefront church—although the original shop was closed in 1963 with founder Frieda Loehmann's death the previous year. Shopping at Loehmann's was an unforgettable experience for any woman. If you were into fashionable clothes at bargain prices, you just had to drop in, and drop in, and drop in. You never knew what you'd

Whoever it was who neatly boarded up these tenements along Fourth Avenue in Gowanus forgot to label the ground floor storefronts with "Post No Bills" signs. As a result we have an inadvertent index to Brooklyn's local movie theaters, thanks to this Berenice Abbott 1936 photo.

find. The really good stuff was on the second floor. All over the ground floor, women of all ages and sizes were frantically trying on whatever caught their fancy. There were no fitting rooms. To a boyfriend or husband trying to look nonchalant at the head of the stairs, the scene was something out of the *Decameron*. For female shoppers, there was always the satisfaction of knowing that all around you almost everyone's thighs looked fatter than yours.

Shopping could be as enjoyable for youngsters as for adults or families. Ask any Brooklyn kids in the days before you needed a car to go to Kings Plaza Shopping Center, and they would have told you that going to a local store could be fun. From the start, being asked to run errands at a nearby shop placed a new mantle of responsibility upon a youth's frail shoulders. It combined the "drudgery" of the trek to the store—as often as not interrupting some game or other ("Now, Ma?" *"Now,* Chris.")—with an awareness that one was beginning to be trusted to undertake things that were normally entrusted to adults.

In the days before the prevalence of the supermarket, every residential neighborhood had its own oasis of local shops. They huddled together, usually anchored at the corner by a grocery or drugstore in the older neighborhoods, or, in the newer, outer areas of Brooklyn, by the corner candy store. Food was, understandably, the staple, and so, alongside the grocer, there was also a fruit-and-vegetable store, a meat market, a fish store. More often then than now, predominantly ethnic neighborhoods had a bakery that featured the specialties of their particular group. Bagels, for example, were not the soft, overly sweet, ubiquitous item of today. They were gray, chewy—verging on impenetrable—and, like bialies, known only in Jewish sections. Italian bread (who heard from French?) was a treat found in an Italian section. It didn't come in a preprinted paper sleeve. Same with Middle Eastern *pita,* Norwegian *fyrstekake,* Swedish *limpa,* or Danish *Helenesnitter.* Bakeries were a necessity for stuffing the children of parents who believed that weight meant health. Lucullus, on Franklin Avenue above Eastern Parkway, was a well-named pastry shop; La Rinascente at 248 Fifth Avenue, among others, dispensed Italian pastry of quality. There were chains such as Cushman's Sons and Hanscom; even though Ebinger's shops were part of a chain, the quality of their pastries was remarkably high. Remember their chocolate blackout cake? Mmmmmmmm.

Some ethnic neighborhoods had stores that were extra-special. Every German and Scandinavian enclave had at least one store

that offered all kinds of delicacies derived from old-country rec-
ipes—hence the name "deli." Every Jewish neighborhood had a
deli too—a delicatessen—but the fare was totally different. No
ham. No shrimp salad. Instead, frankfurters and knishes being
grilled in the window, row after row of mouth-watering smoked
meats, trays of garnishes, bottles of soda and beer. (How come
beer was okay in the deli, but vaguely sinful in the bar and grill?)

Many of these neighborhood shopping areas also had a sampling
of other stores, as well. A drugstore or a Chinese hand laundry
or a tailor shop—the dry-cleaning equipment was always explod-
ing—or a shoemaker (who repaired but rarely *made* shoes, but
the name stuck). The swirling red-striped sidewalk pole announced a barbershop. Beauty parlors, as they were then called,
began to emerge only as wages improved and surplus income
began to accumulate, allowing marginally middle-class women to
seek perms and sets. Their proprietors had to watch out for
wholesale cosmetics salesmen, who had a habit of "accidentally"
breaking things if they didn't place an order for their brand of
merchandise. Unisex? Hardly likely. Barbershops featured violent
arguments over the Dodgers, Giants, and Yankees, and copies of
Sporting News and *The Police Gazette*. (*Playboy* wouldn't appear
regularly until 1954.) Even more common were the tattered copies of the night-before's owl editions of the *News* or *Mirror,* their
outer pages and centerfolds printed on distinctive pink paper. In
beauty parlors, women relaxing under the streamlined, bullet-
shaped hair dryers would gossip about the latest doings on the
block.

In some places the corner store—certainly after Prohibition
ended—became the bar and grill where men at the bar nursed
glasses of Schaefer, Rheingold, Piel's, or Trommer's (also sold in
quarts, "long necks," "steinies," and cans), and women, for the
most part, entered through the side door marked FAMILY
ENTRANCE, usually to have a drink and a meal at a table in the rear.

Every once in a while someone would enter carrying a heavy glass pitcher and shortly emerge with it even heavier, filled to the brim with a white-frothed amber brew delivered "on tap" and covered with a towel to protect it from the inevitable sootfall. To this day, there are those who swear by beer on tap.

In Brooklyn, as in much of urbanized America, mythology celebrates the old corner grocer. Supermarkets spawned by the automobile-dependent suburbs had no standing before the war. Brooklyn did have its A&Ps, and its home-grown chains of Bohack's and Roulston's, but these were hardly supermarkets; they were just chain grocers, each unit small in scale and neat in appearance.

The more interesting and shaggier groceries were "mom and pops" (though we never called them that), those run by families who often lived squeezed into little apartments either behind or over the store. The stores' outsides had a character all their own, like that of the shoemaker next door, with its distinctive plaid show-window decals provided by O'Sullivan's Cat's Paw heels. Grocery windows in those days often had crisp white porcelain letters masticked to the outside of the glass: SALADA TEA. The store itself had gray marble countertops chilly to the touch, oiled wooden floors (there was no asphalt tile), and the warm hue of incandescent lights that didn't reveal how dim they were until the postwar deluge of fluorescents wiped out much of the difference between night and day.

Groceries in those days were different. Like beer, milk too came with a "head," a head of cream, which, being lighter, floated to the top and was skimmed off to be whipped and such. In the twenties and thirties, grocery-store milk was also sold "loose," ladled with a long-handled dipper, officially calibrated at one pint, from giant nickel-plated multigallon containers that now adorn the porches of suburban homes. You brought your own container, and the price was lower than the bottled variety. In places closer to the dairies themselves—less prosperous areas usually—kids would be sent direct, to have their tins filled for a few cents less to quench the thirst of their brothers and sisters. Butter was carved to order from circular wooden tubs (which nestled on their side in the glass-fronted icebox showcase) and then weighed on a sheet of wax paper placed on a scale. Cheese was sold the same way, and cheese boxes, of thin wood, were great to make toys of, or to store things in. ("Hey, Mr. Mullensky! Ya got any cheese boxes today?")

With the art of packaging yet to be perfected, grocery stores smelled richly of the products they purveyed. There was still some unwrapped soap. There was real rye and pumpernickel bread, in addition to Bond, Golden Crust, and Tip Top. There were smoked cold cuts and pungent cheeses. And there was the smell of coffee being ground, skizzing down from its half-ellipsoidal shiny steel container through the dark red electric grinder.

Using a thick-leaded pencil (kept behind his ear), the grocer would tally the prices on the side of a brown paper bag plucked from the stack under the counter—he almost always knew the right size for the "order." Once the addition was done (and re-checked by adding *up* the column) he would lift his fingers like a concert pianist's and press down a group of keys, ringing up the total on his ornate, manually operated, cast-iron-and-bronze National Cash Register, one that neither buzzed, beeped, nor hummed. *Gzing-GZING* went the register, up into its glass-faced top went the numerical total (or sometimes an orange NO SALE tab, when you were getting a deposit back on your returns), and out popped the wood-slatted cash drawer. Half-dollars and silver dollars would first be bounced on the marble counter; a distinctive thud would reveal any counterfeits. And change would be carefully counted out into the customer's hand—as it still is today, in many rural parts of America—coin by coin, bill by bill. A dollar meant something in those days.

The best part of the grocery was the show window. With the end of Prohibition, beer companies vied with one another to dec-orate grocers' show windows with elaborate displays of their prod-ucts. With the coming of pasteurization, preservatives, and dependable packaging, beers were less distinctive in taste from one another, and other considerations than mere flavor had to be employed to lure new customers. Every month or so, a window trimmer in the employ of a beer company would arrive at the store and dismantle the previous month's display, either his own com-pany's or a competitor's. Then, unfolding free-standing, four-color printed posterboards and stretched crepe paper (pronounced "cray paper"), he would decorate the window to feature his com-pany's latest beer promotion. The window trimmers were lithe men who could move gracefully around the show window's cramped spaces without knocking out the plate glass. Their imple-ments were a slender magnetic hammer and a mouthful of blue-steel upholsterer's tacks. It was a miracle they didn't swallow them. They would stretch the crepe paper in tight folds until it was on the verge of tearing, and then, deftly placing magnetized hammerhead to lips, remove a tack and nail the crepe paper in place with one blow. Then they would cover the tack heads with little rosettes of colored paper fashioned, like magic, by their adept fingers. In what seemed like no time the display was done, with bottles and cans and life-sized color pictures all in place, and the trimmer gone. All the grocer had to do then was to wipe the noseprints of the curious children from the outside of the window.

But wait, what was happening now? The grocer was dismantling the display—at least the movable parts. And now he, like the window trimmer before him, was easing his way into the window to add to the display his latest specials of the month: Del Monte tomato paste, Bernice fruit cocktail, Krasdale whole-kernel corn, or S&W olives (colossal). The cans and jars were meticulously arranged in little architectural groupings, some with a topping of one precariously balanced at an angle designed to catch a passer-by's attention. Last came the placing of the plastic price tags: "5 lbs./$1.00," "7 cents—3/20¢," "SPECIAL 2/25¢." Then the placards and beer bottles were replaced, so as not to offend the beer company and to ensure a replacement display next month, when the sunlight would have faded the colors of the paper, and water from the leaky windows would have stained the posters.

Groceries were one thing, stores that sold produce quite another. The English had a simple name for them, one that never arrived with the Pilgrims: "greengrocers." In Brooklyn, the term "fruit store" had to suffice. But what they lacked in a proper name, they made up in the quality of their displays—grandstands of color spilling out across the sidewalk, adding freshness and light to the drabness of the street. Almost everything came in a distinctive container—such as the asparagus box that looked like a smaller-scaled, better-made orange crate, with trapezoidal wooden ends. Fruits were held in particular esteem, many wrapped separately for protection in colored glazed papers printed with individual trademarks—Blue Goose and Indian River oranges stand out, but Anjou pears and pineapples do as well. And on the ground lay wide red rubber bands that had encircled bunches of asparagus, and vivid orange mesh bags in which the onions had arrived.

To us kids, however, the greatest value of these stores lay in their recyclables, such as the two-compartment orange crate that became a lemonade stand in the warm-weather—after the ugly paper labels were scratched off, of course. In the winter they became dollhouses. A cherry box nailed upright to a two-by-four, with half an old roller skate at each end, became a serviceable scooter (sometimes called a pushmobile) as soon as a pair of handles could be nailed to the top. Peach baskets, the tall narrow ones, after their bottoms were knocked out, became vernacular basketball baskets, whether or not their use was Naismith's inspiration. Slats liberated from other crates, when properly nailed together, became play rifles to echo the exploits of Red Ryder or the Lone Ranger or marines in the Solomon Islands.

After the war, when youth gangs multiplied rapidly, the mortise-and-tenoned joint from the end of a lettuce crate (when fastened to a piece of hollow car antenna with some thick rubber bands and a healthy dose of hostility) became the feared "zip gun" that snuffed out all too many teenagers' lives.

Each type of food store had its idiosyncrasy. Sawdust identified those selling meats and fish. Before we knew of chipboard or Masonite, wood was the seemingly unlimited, easily worked, and therefore cheap staple of construction. The inevitable byproduct, sawdust, became the cheapest means to absorb a floor's dampness or grease, making for easy cleaning. Sweep out the sawdust, and

The surface of Neptune Avenue between Brighton 3rd and 4th streets was largely mud but the tradition of hanging out in front of the candy store newsstand had already been firmly established in 1932 by the neighborhood "boys."

out too went the drippings and the droppings. Among the messiest memories of childhood is a butcher's floor on a snowy day, when the sawdust piled higher and higher. It came to resemble the floor of a stable, until closing time allowed a thorough sweep-up. And in the summer there was the periodic—and not often enough—disposal of the butcher shop's waste meat and fat for rendering into soap. In the midday heat, their vile smell called attention to the big blue trucks of the Van Iderstine Company. Why they were painted navy blue, which only contributed to their absorption of solar radiation and added to the stench of the rotting waste, was hard to comprehend. So was the idea that the driver was really able to keep from retching.

It may not have sold the necessities of life, but a candy store was the true anchor of a Brooklyn neighborhood. Overhead was a sign extorted by (from) an ice cream company—Horton's or Reid's or Breyer's. Or one provided by a cigar wholesaler—Optimo or Natural Bloom or Max Schwartz's La Primadora Havana Cigars. It was often an impromptu center of neighborhood communication; when home telephones were not—and pay phones along the curb hardly existed at all—as commonplace as today, calls placed to the candy store telephone booth would get you a two- or three-cent tip for running a message to a neighbor wanted on the phone. In front of the store, the sidewalk was tattooed by irregular black splotches—used chewing gum—and the asphalt beyond was ornamented by soda-bottle caps pressed into its surface by passing vehicles.

Outside was a newsstand that displayed an array of newspapers under sashweights to keep them from blowing away. There were so many, both morning and afternoon, that there were always fights among the delivery men as to the proper protocol of display. In the early morning (and in the late evening, when the pink-paper "owl" editions appeared with baseball scores) the *Daily News* fought the *Daily Mirror;* the *Times* fought the *Herald Tribune.* After lunch the battle was between the *Post,* the *Sun,* the *Journal-American,* and the *World-Telegram.* For a time, Ralph Ingersoll's *P.M.* joined the circulation follies. And don't forget Brooklyn's own *Brooklyn Eagle* and, briefly, the *Brooklyn Daily Times,* as well. Most of the borough's newsstands were spiced by at least one of the city's foreign-language papers. Today they're barely weeklies; they were dailies then. The Yiddish *Forward, Il Progresso Italiano, Staats-Zeitung,* and the Russian-language *Novoye Russkoye Slovo,* whose Cyrillic lettering made the kids think it was read by HOBOES. Adding color were the magazines—*Life* and *Look, Liberty* and *Collier's, Popular Mechanics* and *The Saturday Evening Post.* And for the kids, there were the comic books featuring Nancy and Little Lulu, Superman and Batman and Plastic Man, and Wonder Woman.

Once inside, an unforgettable aroma enveloped you—a mixture of candy, cigarettes, cedarwood cigar boxes and their contents, paper goods, and printing ink not quite dry from the dailies, weeklies, and monthlies constantly turning over in the rhythm of business.

The mainstay of the candy store, of course, was sweets. Lollipops for the little ones, nickel candy bars in glossy wrappers (like Baby Ruths or Butterfingers) were for the big kids. Long, salted pretzels were largely for the adults, who consumed them with their egg creams or malteds. (Another favored accompaniment was Drake's pound cake, toasted in its cellophane wrapper—who knows why it didn't catch fire?—and then sliced in half.) In warm weather there were frozen Milky Ways, kept in the freezer alongside the ice cream until rock-hard. And there was also something called penny candy, in a wide array to tempt kids as their bribe for getting through another day of school, or whatever. Usually it was displayed on tiers of glass shelves in the back of the store, in a slope-fronted glass case just the right height for the typical penny-candy customer, aged seven to ten. (The store-fixture designers of that time really knew their trade; they should be designing museum displays today.) The various kinds of penny candies must have had names, but they were selected by simply catching the eye of the candy-store man (or his wife) and pointing. Some seasons were gripped by candy fads, like the long paper strips resembling adding-machine tapes and "printed" with rows of colored sugar "buttons" that you bit off, one by one, with your front teeth. Or the grotesque, lipstick-red wax lips that you clenched between your teeth—the ones that gave some boys their first taste of drag—and which some even chewed when they became soft: "It's wax. *Eeuucccch!*"

And as you left, you had to have a piece of bubble gum, Fleer's, with the wax-paper color comics looking as if they'd been printed by a microscope. The latter rarely satisfied, but they were an integral part of the time-consuming process of gum-softening. What else could you do while your molars were crushing the hard pink blob but read the cartoon and try out the halfhearted riddles on your friends?

What really made a candy store a candy store, in point of fact, was what was called the "spa" in less urbanized places than Brooklyn—the soda fountain, or simply the "fountain." In that era before Formica, fountains were of a pinkish gray marble and had before them a row of hard wood-and-cast-iron revolving seats, each with a bronze footrest. The woodwork behind the fountain was dark, in some hybrid walnut-mahogany stain, with glass doors behind which were school supplies that doubled for what grownups called "stationery," those rare times your folks decided they had to write a letter. (Every candy-store man was a self-appointed postmaster, selling postage stamps at cost and offering advice about when to use Special Delivery.) Envelopes were sold one at a time for a penny apiece; so were cigarettes, for that matter—a penny apiece for those who couldn't afford a whole pack. Johnny—the dapper little bellboy—stepped out of thousands of store windows and counters all over Brooklyn, crying, "Call . . . for . . .Phil-ip . . . Morr-eess." A brand called Wings continued an old tradition: cigarette cards, which some collected as avidly as others did postage stamps. A postcard rack on the wall held a selection of local scenes printed on linen-textured card stock in totally unreal colors, also at a penny apiece. Who wanted to send anyone a card from *there?*

Every fountain had three chromium-plated brass spigots, with black Bakelite handles. The center one dispensed tap water. But the other two shpritzed cold seltzer, the elixir of Brooklyn's candy stores. A 2¢ plain, immortalized by Harry Golden, was a large glass seltzer; a 1¢ plain ("penny plain") was a small. Fruit drinks tasted best when they were made from syrups displayed in wrinkly glass containers of a polyhedral form that, to this day, defies appellation. As with the spigots, there were three such containers, holding a green (lemon-and-lime flavor), a red (cherry), and an orange (you guessed it) syrup that, when mixed with seltzer, created a soda (a "pop" or "phosphate" to foreigners from upstate or other wildernesses).

On special occasions, an ice-cream soda was in order: all vanilla, all chocolate, or black-and-white. Ice cream at the candy store was different from Good Humors, Eskimo Pies, or Bungalow Bars. There was more variety, since it was more or less scooped (except for prewrapped, cylindrical Mel-o-Rols and their specially shaped cake cups) from multigallon cartons to make cones, sundaes, frappés, and malteds. Why was it that the distinctive Hamilton Beach malted machines were then a monopoly among candy stores?

Today it's hard to find a real fountain. If you want a soda, you order a Coke, premixed. The bright red countertop Coke dispenser simply didn't exist before the war, and so Cokes were actually mixed by hand, from Coca-Cola Company syrup and seltzer. That's how the cherry Coke or the vanilla Coke emerged, products of the combined imagination of soda jerk and customer. A product also of that same combined imagination must have been the egg cream, a mixture of chocolate syrup, milk, and seltzer. Lost to historians—but claimed by many—is knowledge of precisely when—and where—this concoction first appeared. It is even unclear whether it ever had either egg or cream in it. But a candy store minus an egg cream, in Brooklyn at least, was as difficult to conceive of as the earth without gravity.

Just "hangin' around" in Johnny Sanservino's one-table pool hall on President Street in 1936. Notice the bent wire chairs that one also found in barber shops and ice-cream parlors.

11

CHICKEE—D' COPS!

he score was 6 to 5 and it was getting dark, too dark for another inning, at least in *this* stickball game. It was two out, a man on first, and the losing team was up. There were few cars along the curbs, and none could be seen coming up the block, so Mootchy stepped up to home plate, the manhole cover with the hexagon pattern and the BPB monogram on it—Borough President of Brooklyn. Everyone knew that behind Mootchy's calm lay the strength of a horse, and a homer would win the game. He bounced the Spaldeen a couple of times and then swung the bat with all his might. *Thwock!* He did it! Look at that ball go!

Crash! The sound of splintering glass, and then the voice of the indignant householder: "I'm calling the police."

"Chickee—d' cops!"

The traditional cry on Brooklyn's streets that meant it was time to scatter and to worry about the Law's questions later.

Despite the panicked departure of many on sneakered feet, there were always the few—some with bravado, others with innocence—who hung around waiting for the police prowl car to arrive. Unless there was a broom-handle bat to retrieve, the cop never emerged from his car, then usually a two-tone, two-door, two-seat Plymouth coupe. There was only one cop per car back then, and he was lucky—he could've been assigned to foot patrol!

The courageous ones hunched over the police car, asses out, elbows on the sill of the car window, to have a mature face-to-face with the mock-serious officer. The guys who stayed always had

The Police Department's detectives and federal agents from Washington didn't fool around, with gangs like Murder, Inc. in operation. This display of armament was intended to make the obvious point.

some baloney to pass on to the cop, about their own innocence and the evident guilt of those who had run away (and who looked on from behind nearby bushes and doorways). The conversation always took longer than you could stand. What were they saying? Was the cop taking names and addresses? Which of them was squealing?

For most Brooklyn kids, this was about the extent of their contact with the Law. While the arrival of the cops happened more often than desired, the experience rarely resulted in more than a mild reprimand, first from the cop, and then, as the gossip rippled down the block in ever-widening circles, from parents. In many areas there were "beat cops," uniformed police who walked the same route regularly. They knew *everything*. And if you really made a pest of yourself they wouldn't bother to boot you in the can, they'd just go talk to your folks. Then you'd *really* get it!

But for some Brooklynites, contact with cops was an everyday fact of life. For one thing, there seemed to be more cops then. Severe problems never seemed to tax the uniformed police. "Call out the reserves!" was the favored command reported in the press in those days. Nevertheless, in a place with a population of better than two million, there were a lot of people to prey upon and many illegal services to provide, temptations that some of Brooklyn's citizens simply couldn't resist. And chances were that those running the numbers or taking the bets or perpetrating the scams had to answer to the cops at least some of the time, if not necessarily to pay the consequences.

Take Prohibition, for example. The national ban on the manufacture, sale, and transportation of liquor went into effect at midnight on January 16, 1920, and set the stage for a special period in America's—and Brooklyn's—history. In came the Roaring Twenties, the Jazz Age, and the nationwide corporate interlock of the underworld.

Brooklyn had three vital resources that clashed with the supposed national fervor to dry up the land: a lot of thirsty people, its own ocean coastline (as well as easy access to the rest of Long Island's), and a wonderful tradition of beer-brewing resident in a large inventory of old breweries. The last allowed the local, large-scale manufacture of "home brews," provided you had the right connections and knew whose palm required greasing so the authorities would look the other way.

While Manhattan's speakeasies were better known than those across the river, those in Brooklyn weren't far behind. Every week, newspapers noted the raiding of illicit speaks like the Bedford Nest, at 1286 Bedford Avenue, considered by the press to be Brooklyn's most palatial, Oetjen's at Church and Flatbush, across from the Flatbush Theatre, or the Red Hook Lane Restaurant, located on Court Square right next door to Kings County's Democratic headquarters. Nor were Brooklyn's better-known restaurants and nightclubs models of compliance. The Marine Roof of the Bossert Hotel, in the Heights, was one of the city's hottest night spots, enjoying the title "the Waldorf of Brooklyn." During Prohibition it was impossible to get onto the roof without a reservation. The big bands played. Rudy Vallee sang. The beautiful people came. And liquor flowed.

At least some of Brooklyn's illegal hootch came in via rumrunners operating along Brooklyn's miles of South Shore waters and the remainder of the island's lengthy and difficult-to-patrol shoreline.

From well back in the nineteenth century, Kings County was one of the nation's leading beer-brewing centers. Brooklyn had a considerable German immigrant population that constituted a large market with a taste for lager. And its Irish population, also extensive, found the local ales and porters to its liking as well. Before the era of mechanical refrigeration and the widespread use of preservatives, beers didn't travel well, and so brewers and their customers had to be in close proximity. As a result, Brooklyn abounded in breweries. With the advent of Prohibition, which only allowed the brewing of near-beer, Brooklyn's beer manufactories were faced with disaster. Under the Volstead Act, only cereal beverages containing less than .5 percent alcohol could be sold. That meant they had to have less alcohol than sauerkraut. (Ever try tying one on with sauerkraut?)

Oetjen's Restaurant at 2210 Church Avenue was one of Brooklyn's most fashionable, located near the intersection with Flatbush Avenue. On July 21, 1930, it was raided for the third time by Prohibition agents, and six men were arrested. Illegal liquor flowed as freely in Brooklyn as it did elsewhere.

Some breweries used their extensive plumbing to make bottled sodas, while others succumbed to making the watered-down, legal version of suds. These ghost breweries were the ones whose equipment was quietly recycled to produce the illegal liquor that made Prohibition such a hotbed of crime.

One such ghost was apparently the Excelsior Brewing Company at 277–279 Pulaski Street. Prohibition had not treated Excelsior well, and by 1923 the company had sold its holdings. The new owners seemed content to brew near-beer, despite the less-than-fervent demand for the stuff.

On August 7, 1930, Prohibition agents raided the nearby Hercules Express Company garage on DeKalb Avenue, a couple of blocks from the Excelsior facilities. There they found ten moving vans, their side panels painted to look as if they were from out of town. Eight were filled with empty beer kegs, two with portable filling equipment. Although the agents found no beer, they did find a pipe that they traced to another garage on Pulaski Street, just across from Excelsior. In that structure they found two pipes, one that led back to Hercules and one that they surmised led to the brewery across the way. Later, with the help of police "reserves," they dug up the pipe that crossed Pulaski Street, but couldn't gain access to the brewery itself, so the Feds seized the place instead and arrested the new owners.

Unfortunately, Prohibition's own Catch-22 voided the whole proceeding. To enter a suspected premises legally, one needed a search warrant; to get a search warrant, one needed evidence obtained from the premises. Sure enough, a few months later a federal judge threw out the whole case.

The nationwide scope of Prohibition and the large scale of the illegal activities it engendered set the stage for the corporate unification of separate criminal gangs in exactly the same way that gangs had earlier ended the rugged individualism of solo criminals. The organization of underworld activities in the image of American corporate big business was called variously "the Crime Trust," "the Syndicate," or "the Combination." All across the land the Syndicate, via regional divisions, took over, exercising control over bootlegging, gambling, narcotics, prostitution, numbers, slot machines, loansharking, and certain union locals.

From such activities in New York City emerged a figure who would place his name—and Brooklyn's—on the national map, alongside Bonnie and Clyde, Dillinger, and Pretty Boy Floyd. His

The makers of Trommer's Beer were among many happy brewers when Prohibition was repealed in 1933. Here a Mack Bulldog truck is about to depart from the brewery with a load of kegs for the thirsty patrons of Brooklyn's neighborhood taverns.

name was Louis "Lepke" Buchalter, a carpetbagging native of the Lower East Side. Reflecting a partnership in the Ocean Hill and Brownsville communities with another thug, Jacob "Gurrah" Shapiro, the team was known as "L & G"—for Lepke and Gurrah— which soon became as familiar a trademark on the New York crime scene as A & P and P & G were in the grocery business. Buchalter's nickname derived from his Hebrew name *Layb* (for "lion") which was anglicized to "Louis" on his birth certificate. At home and on the streets he was commonly addressed by a diminutive, Layb'l, or Layb'ke. The latter, poorly transliterated by a tin-eared press into "Lepke," emerged as the name that would become notorious. Partner Shapiro's moniker came from his favorite ejaculation, "Get ourra hir!" usually uttered in a guttural rasp, hence "Gurrah." These two and their boys were regarded as among the twenties' and thirties' most aggressive, brutal, and successful teams of gangsters. Their specialty was industrial and labor racketeering, and they held control over New York's baking, flour-trucking, dressmaking, fur, and men's garment industries. The racketeering, however, was not what was to command the national headlines, but L & G's sideline, the professionalized contract extermination of troublemakers for the mob.

In 1935, at the zenith of their career, L & G's illegal activities were recognized by New York's popular Democratic governor, Herbert H. Lehman. To clean up the pervasive racketeering in which they excelled, he appointed the young, fastidious, and politically ambitious Republican attorney, Thomas E. Dewey. As special prosecutor, Dewey showed outspoken determination to pursue Lepke as the local symbol of lawlessness. This had the effect of publicizing Lepke's nationwide enforcement/extermination squad, which came to be known, in the colorful words of *New York World-Telegram* reporter Henry Feeny, as "Murder, Inc."

As a result of the well-publicized activities of the Lepke-Gurrah mob in the 1930s, Brownsville became identified with organized crime. This 1936 scene at Sutter Avenue looking east past Ralph looks very calm, but . . .

It was the gang's meeting place in Brownsville that was to enter the name of Brooklyn rapidly and immortally into the annals of American crime.

At "Midnight Rose's," a candy store at the corner of Livonia and Saratoga avenues, the gang conferred over long pretzels and egg creams, planning the strategy that gained it control of Brooklyn's lucrative rackets while pursuing a brutal enforcement role across the forty-eight states. Lepke's men made quite a roster: Abraham "Kid Twist" Reles, Harry "Happy" Maione, Hershel "Pittsburgh Phil" Strauss, Frank "the Dasher" Abbendado, Mot'l "Bugsy" Goldstein, Anthony "the Duke" Maffetore, Abraham "Pretty" Levine, Philip "Little Farfel" Cohen, Irving "Knadles" Nitzberg, and Albert "Allie Tick Tock" Tannenbaum. These prize executioners, the staff of Murder, Inc., traveled the country fulfilling the contracts arranged by the various branches of the Combination. It is said that they were responsible for a thousand gangland executions, among them those undertaken for Lepke and Gurrah of individuals they feared might sing to Dewey's staff.

Meanwhile, L & G were being hounded for lesser transgressions. Already appealing a conviction by a federal court—for Sherman Antitrust Law violations, would you believe?—but fearing Dewey's fanaticism and threats even more, Lepke and Gurrah went into hiding—in Flatbush, they say—in the spring of 1937. From his local exile, Lepke continued to direct the extermination of former associates who might testify against the pair. Between 1935 and 1939, some thirteen persons were professionally wiped out in Lepke's attempt to rewrite his personal history. Then, after Dewey narrowly missed winning the governorship (his new visibility caused him to lose by only 1.5 percent of the vote, 12,000 ballots), the two fugitives gave themselves up—first the sickly Gurrah, on April 14, 1938, then, on August 24, 1939, Lepke himself. The latter, fearing Dewey's vindictiveness, chose to surrender to the FBI. Discounting the warnings of his associate, Albert "the Executioner" Anastasia, Lepke was persuaded by Morris "Moey Dimples" Wolensky—no relation to the author— that the Feds, as part of Roosevelt's Democratic administration, would never turn him over to Dewey, a potential Republican presidential rival.

They did.

Dewey lost no time placing Lepke on trial in Manhattan for extortion and other noncapital crimes for which indictments had been obtained during L & G's exile. But across the river, in Brooklyn, another melodrama was about to begin, this one directed by Kings County's new district attorney, William O'Dwyer.

It was 1940 and O'Dwyer, a proven vote-getter with his eye on the mayoralty, had just stepped into the Brooklyn District Attorney's scandal-ridden office. As ambitious in his own way as Dewey, O'Dwyer was also looking to develop a record of achievement with which to further his political ambitions. Reviving the investigation of a long-unsolved killing, O'Dwyer was able to dig up barely enough evidence to charge a trio of Murder, Inc., henchmen with first-degree murder. One of them, the aforementioned Abe "Kid Twist" Reles, was a trusted, highly placed Lepke lieutenant, whose wife was pregnant at the time. To avoid the electric chair, Reles surprised everyone by turning state's evidence, using his photographic memory to develop a confession that not only filled thousands of pages but implicated Lepke in murder. Murder. Lepke's number was up. Where the Feds and the state had failed, William O'Dwyer—despite much *kuhnk'l-muhnk'l* that had gone on in his office—succeeded. In April 1941, he was able to indict Louis Lepke Buchalter, together with a group of Murder, Inc., gunsels, for a capital crime—first-degree murder.

The trial itself didn't begin until the summer, and by then O'Dwyer was running—unsuccessfully—for the mayoralty against LaGuardia, thus excusing himself from the task of actually prosecuting the case. You could lose friends that way.

Lepke was found guilty and, many years later, was actually executed for the crime in Sing Sing's electric chair, but not before a curious occurrence involving key witness Kid Twist Reles.

During the Lepke trial, Reles and the other witnesses were sequestered for safekeeping in the Half Moon Hotel, on the Boardwalk at West Twenty-ninth within view of Coney Island's roller coasters. Reles and the others were in a sixth-floor suite behind an iron door and under twenty-four-hour-a-day guard by five cops under the command of Police Captain Frank C. Bals. Everyone agreed that Reles was in safe hands. "The bird can sing," they were saying about stool pigeon Reles, "but he can't fly."

But somehow, despite all the precautions, Reles tried. His broken body was found early on the morning of Wednesday, November 12, 1941, lying on the roof of the Half Moon's kitchen. Wafting in the ocean breezes from his open bedroom window, five floors up, were some wire and a few bedsheets that had been tied together. How had Reles died? Where were the cops during all this? (Sleeping, all five of them sheepishly admitted later, just before they were demoted.) What did Captain Bals have to say?

A decade later—after enjoying a brief elevation to seventh deputy police commissioner by Mayor O'Dwyer—Bals explained to Senator Kefauver's Crime Investigating Committee that he believed Reles, bored to tears and finding his guardians asleep, tried to lower himself to the next floor so he could surprise them all by knocking on their door. All for laughs, Bals said. The committee thought otherwise. New Hampshire's dour Senator Charles Tobey found Bals's story hard to swallow: "O. Henry, in all his wonderful moments, never conceived of such a wonderful, silly story as this."

A convincing explanation has still not emerged, although later, Lucky Luciano claimed that Bals and his men had received $50,000 to heave Reles out of the window and tie the bedsheets together. But who could believe Lucky Luciano?

Perhaps the only lesson to be learned from all of this is what

This idyllic 1935 scene along the Coney Island Boardwalk shows the Half Moon Hotel before it gained notoriety when the state's witness against Murder, Inc., Abe Reles, mysteriously died in a fall from his sixth floor room, where he was being guarded by police.

the smart alecks in Brooklyn's candy stores said at the time, as they munched their long pretzels and savored their egg creams: "The only law Kid Twist could understand was the law of gravity."

Looking the other way was also something not unheard of among Brooklyn's law enforcement agencies. By 1950, when O'Dwyer was about to begin his second term as mayor, a scandal erupted that started to reveal how closely crime and law enforcement could cooperate, especially in Kings County.

On December 4th of that year, Kings County's District Attorney Miles F. McDonald arraigned an individual named Harry Gross, together with thirty others, for bookmaking. (McDonald had been an assistant DA on O'Dwyer's staff, back when he had been busy pursuing Murder, Inc.) McDonald charged Gross with being the kingpin in a ten-year-old, $20-million-a-year bookmaking and gambling operation in which at least $1 million a year in "ice" was paid to the police. The grand jury's investigation was prompted by a series of front-page exposés by investigative reporter Ed Reid in the *Brooklyn Eagle*.

Shortly after his arraignment, Gross pleaded guilty to sixty-six counts of bookmaking—which could have meant sixty-six years' imprisonment—and agreed to become the key witness in the criminal trial of a score of plainclothes police and high brass, whom he had identified behind the grand jury's closed doors.

At the last moment, however, claiming threats to himself and his family, and with rumors also flying of a $75,000 bribe, Gross sabotaged the trial. Despite his earlier promise, he refused to identify the police he had named to the grand jury. For this and other contempts of court, he was sentenced to 1,800 days in jail and a $15,000 fine, to which later was added a twelve-year sentence for his earlier bookmaking admissions. But he cost the district attorney his case, and on September 19, 1951, with tears streaming from his eyes, DA McDonald moved to dismiss the indictments against the accused cops.

Now deeply embarrassed by almost two years of front-page headlines—the *Eagle*'s reporter had by now won at least three coveted journalism awards for the inquiry stories—the Police Department proceeded to conduct its own departmental trial. It was the largest ever in New York City history, and took place in December 1951 in the old, almost forgotten, third-floor courtroom of Brooklyn's Borough Hall. With no witnesses like Gross to finger them, only nine of the original thirty defendants were found guilty

of departmental allegations. Their penalty: dismissal from the force. Another, the highest police official ever tried, an assistant chief inspector, was demoted to captain. He filed for retirement (at his previous post's higher pay scale) within hours.

The department's real losses from the lengthy probe, however, were grimly related in a *New York Times* editorial the next day. Gone from police ranks were a commissioner, a chief of detectives, a chief inspector, three deputy chief inspectors, four inspectors, one deputy inspector, three captains, and scores of plainclothesmen. The higher-ups were forced to resign, many of the others retired early, some were found guilty of perjury or lesser charges such as conduct unbecoming an officer, and some even went to prison. A few took their own lives.

William O'Dwyer had meanwhile become Ambassador to Mexico.

After a few months behind bars, Gross relented and decided he'd better testify, if only to make a deal to shorten his sentence. During his first appearance, he summed up his career as Brooklyn's bookmaking kingpin with these immortal words: "I paid everybody. Everybody."

The yard of the Brooklyn City Prison, at what was once 149 Raymond Street, nuzzled against the western slope of Fort Greene Park. After the street name was changed to Ashland Place, the facility continued to be referred to as "The Raymond Street Jail." The photograph dates from 1942.

12

TODAY'S A DAY FOR THE BEACH

To most people, Memorial Day—or Decoration Day, as it was called then—was just a day off from the drudgery of work. Families might use it to decorate the graves of loved ones killed in the Great War. Others looked forward to watching the neighborhood parades. But to many a Brooklynite, that particular day off was important for another reason. May 30th meant that Coney Island had officially opened again for another summer's fun.

The arrival of the last of the four subway trunk lines at the Stillwell Avenue station in 1920 had a vast democratizing influence over who came to Coney. The nickel was the stabilized price for the ride, the hot dog, and the milk shake; and at Nathan's, orange drink could be had for only three cents. Coney Island had become the watering place of *all* the people, not just the select visitors (as had been the case in an earlier era)—scions of high society and patrons of organized vice. The extension of the subway to Coney Island had brought the resort within a nickel's reach of all the city's millions, making it a favored place to take the family for a weekend outing. It came to be called "the Nickel Empire."

A warm summer Sunday in 1900 would attract crowds of 100,000 to the beach, its restaurants, and its hotels—only three percent of the city's 3.4 million population. Many of these were attracted by Coney's nearby racetracks—Brooklyn was then known as the horseracing capital of America. But by 1920, with the arrival of the subway, Sunday attendance was known to rise to more than a million—eighteen percent of the burgeoning city's

Everybody—men, women, and children—wore tank-top swimsuits in this 1925 picture taken from Steeplechase Pier. It wasn't until the thirties that men were permitted to wear just trunks to the beach. Does it look like anyone in the water can swim?

5.6 million population—even though, by then, horseracing in Brooklyn had long since disappeared. Drawn by the waves and rides, larger and larger crowds came until after World War II. The largest Sunday crowd is thought to have been that assembled on July 3, 1947, the last year before the availability of automobiles ineluctably began to lure city-dwelling Americans to the suburbs. It was probably no coincidence that Grand Central Terminal's record for passengers was also reached that same year.

A half-century earlier, in the Gay Nineties, Coney Island's society heyday, gay blades would make a day of it, taking in the Suburban or Futurity Stakes at the Sheepshead Bay Racetrack, or the Preakness at the Gravesend course. They would then drive their trotters to elaborate seaside hostelries to treat their ladies to grouse and champagne at fifty dollars a dinner, quite a sum in those days. For those who liked to feel their pulses quicken at a less fashionable racetrack, there were the races at the old Brighton Beach Fairgrounds. But in 1910, reform was again in the air in Albany, and the state legislators delivered a body blow to the "sport of kings" by enacting strict laws against gambling. Without the chance to gamble, horseracing was robbed of its spice, and Brooklyn's three tracks—Sheepshead Bay, Gravesend, and Brighton Beach—closed, ending the days when they served such flashy figures as William Kissam Vanderbilt, August Belmont, Jr., Leonard W. Jerome, and Harry Payne Whitney. Brooklyn would no longer be known as the horseracing capital of the country.

With racing gone, the owners of the empty courses sought alternative uses. On September 11, 1911, pilot Calbraith P. Rodgers, as part of a publicity effort for a soda pop called "Vin Fiz, The Ideal Grape Drink," lifted his Vin Fiz flyer from the empty infield of the Sheepshead Bay Track to become the first to fly an "aero-plane" coast to coast. In the ensuing years, the tracks at Sheepshead Bay and Brighton Beach became speedways for the racehorse's replacement—gasoline-powered racing cars. And while horseracing also ceased at Gravesend, horses continued to be quartered and trained there to be raced at tracks farther away from Manhattan, in Queens and Nassau counties (tracks that had reopened later in the decade, at sites less accessible—and less valuable—than Brooklyns'). The stand-in uses of the Brooklyn courses were only temporary. With the end of World War I and a steep rise in the city's population, the land under all three Brooklyn tracks gained in value and found its eventual destiny as tracts for residential development. In 1922 the Gravesend site, lying southwest of Ocean Parkway and Kings Highway, became a huge development of houses with Mediterranean tile roofs and stone-urned piazzas. The other two soon followed suit.

The growth of Coney Island's popular appeal went hand-in-hand with the decline of other of its old institutions. The ornate, rambling, wood-frame hotels of the nineteenth century had been built in the same years as the racetracks; all had been in place by the 1880s. These grand old hostelries had had well-appointed rooms and lavish dining accommodations befitting the style of fashionably dressed guests at a "distant" seaside resort. But now, with racing gone, the hotels were no longer fashionable. They were also expensive to operate and maintain.

One by one the caravansaries closed. The exclusive Oriental was demolished in 1916 to provide land for the urbanization of Manhattan Beach. The Manhattan Beach Hotel, opened ceremonially by President Ulysses S. Grant in 1877, was also razed during the teens. The Brighton Beach Hotel, whose buildings rambled across the lands to the west of Coney Island Avenue between the beach and the Brighton Beach elevated station (across from the later Brighton Beach Baths), lasted till 1923. Lesser hotels were the victims of fire and neglect. The Prospect, where motion pictures were first shown in Coney Island, held on until 1935, and the Ravenhall came down that same year, although its name continued to be used for the swimming pool and baths at Surf Avenue and West 19th Street.

In the hotels' early years, visitors from Manhattan had first to take a ferry ride and then complete their journey on a steam train. Now, with the advent of subways, the once-distant seaside had simply become the edge of the five-borough consolidated city. The

needs of the new visitors would be satisfied by day-trip accommodations. With the coming of the automobile, the rich were going elsewhere, even farther away from their city homes. In place of hotels came amenities for the masses, an array of bathhouses.

In the twenties and thirties at least, dress codes at the beach were hardly as liberal as today. It was not until Mayor LaGuardia came out in favor of bare-chested bathing for men, in the thirties, that the exposure of men's nipples did not result in arrest, fines, and the decline of Western Civilization. That era's bathing suits were not only cumbersome but also lacked the quick-drying characteristics conferred by today's synthetic fabrics. Swimsuits covered your torso and then some, tended to become itchy with the infiltration of sand, and just never, never seemed to dry.

Bathhouses were the answer. You could check your wallet and keys and then stuff your clothes into a locker. You could rent—rather than tote from home—whatever you might need on the beach: a suit, wooden clogs, a striped towel, a beach chair or umbrella. Later you could change out of your damp bathing suit and take a bracing cold shower before an evening on Surf Avenue or Coney's Bowery, taking in the rides, the sideshows, and the penny arcades.

The first of the large changing facilities, the Municipal Baths, was a concrete structure built in the early twenties at Surf Avenue and West Fifth Street. Following the city's lead, some thirty privately operated bathhouses—all less substantially built—were put into operation by the end of the decade, linked to one another in 1923 by the opening of Coney Island's spectacular eighty-foot-wide Boardwalk. At first it separated sand from land for 1.8 miles, but eventually was more than doubled in length.

Coney Island's busy Surf Avenue, looking east toward Ocean Parkway in the distance in the early thirties. On the left were the entrance pylons to Luna Park; immediately across the avenue, the block-square Feltman's restaurant complex.

Municipal Baths and Beach, Coney Island, N. Y.

ROLLING CHAIRS ON THE BOARDWALK, CONEY ISLAND, N. Y.

Along the Boardwalk's wooden surface you could walk—watch out for splinters—talk, sit on park benches, or be propelled by a boy pushing one of those romantic wheeled wickerwork contrivances common to most seaside resorts, in this case furnished by Brooklyn's own Boardwalk Rolling Chair Company. It set you back seventy-five cents an hour, plus tip. Feel the vibration of the wheels rumbling on the wooden slats. Underneath, in the secluded, dappled netherworld below the boards, were taking place other activities, more intimate ones, which required the special shaded privacy that the Boardwalk afforded. Some called it the Hotel Underwood; *they* went on to become copywriters on Madison Avenue.

While Coney's grand hotels disappeared, at least one of the finer eateries continued to flourish. Feltman's had originally been the restaurant for Feltman's Ocean Pavilion hotel, opened in 1874. The hotel came down, but the large food establishment remained popular, stretching all the way from the Boardwalk to Surf Avenue, just across from Luna Park. Feltman's wasn't just one restaurant. At its peak, it was an intertwining of two bars and nine restaurants with beautiful gardens, and designated by names like the Wisteria Pergola, the Deutscher Garten, the Garden Club, and the Maple Gardens, each with a live orchestra. As labor costs rose and the affluence of the clientele declined, the accommodations were reduced and a dance floor was installed upstairs. The food was widely hailed and included shore dinners and blue-plate specials. It stopped short of the lowly hot dog on a roll, which Charles Feltman is credited with having invented in his original establishment on Howard Avenue in East New York. Its success had propelled him to Coney.

With the coming of larger and larger crowds, representatives of Manhattan's restaurant chains followed suit. Nedick's hot dog stands came. A Child's Restaurant was erected in a romantic terra-cotta-clad structure at the Boardwalk and West Twenty-first Street, near the Washington Baths. A peek into the automated future was provided Boardwalk strollers by Sodamat, an arcade of gleaming automated devices that dispensed carbonated beverages into cups with the drop of a coin and the push of a button. In the thirties, this was a novelty.

At the southwest corner of Stillwell and Surf avenues, just kitty-corner from the BMT line's terminal, stands Nathan's Famous, looking not terribly different today from the way it did in those days, but considerably expanded. It opened in 1916 at the southeast corner of Schweikert's Walk, the alley between Stillwell Avenue and West Fifteenth Street, by Nathan Handwerker—a latecomer to Coney, compared to Feltman. Everyone else was charging ten cents apiece for frankfurters, but Handwerker decided to reduce his price to a nickel. Feltman's and Nathan's both continued to attract crowds until 1954, when Feltman's closed.

A trip to Coney Island was unforgettable to the hundreds of

Billboards along the Boardwalk, looking west from Stillwell Avenue in July of 1933. The Sodamat was a place that was lined with automatic soda machines that dispensed carbonated beverages in paper cups, in that era still a novelty. The Fisher Bros. clothing store featured on the billboard is today a suburban store in Nassau's Five Towns.

Nathan's original midblock frankfurter stand at Surf Avenue and Schweikert's Walk five years after its opening in 1916. Note that everything cost a nickel: franks, hamburgers, roast beef, beverages. The business did so well that it came to occupy the entire blockfront to the Stillwell Avenue corner.

thousands, the millions, who clogged its sands on hot summer weekends. The rolling lip of cool ocean waves was restrained by stone jetties that divided the beach's length into socially stratified enclaves. The sands were hardly pristine, but with so many people, they weren't often visible. Sanitation was at a minimum, and despite the financial incentives of deposit bottles, broken glass was not unheard of. In the twenties, with lifeguards purely patronage appointees, many chosen for the job could hardly have saved a life in an emergency; some weighed in at more than two hundred pounds, and their ages ranged to sixty. The life-saving dories wound up being used for fishing, even on the most crowded of Sundays. And it was best to keep away from the first-aid shacks; they were used for shacking, all right, by the lifeguards and the loose ladies left over from Saturday-night parties.

With the LaGuardia era came Robert Moses, whose enormous "NO" signs planted on the sands made the beach's innumerable rules of behavior more explicit to those who came there to read, but they hardly made a dent in the condition of the beach. Patronage continued, but the lifeguards got younger. The noise of the crowds and the splashing of the surf were now interrupted by blasts of the lifeguard's whistle and the waving of arms: "Too far out!" "Too close to the rocks!" "Quit the horseplay!" Teenage girls thronged the base of his high wooden chair, looking up worshipfully, some ecstatically. A young, suntanned lifeguard couldn't help but be a special fella.

The amusements, though in use both day and night, took on special significance as the sun began to slip toward the horizon and the tight, hot feel of your skin made it clear that it was time to leave the sand. Millions of individual lightbulbs electrified the scene and special sounds began to fill the air. The mechanical music of the merry-go-rounds played tunes so familiar they didn't need names. The *clackety-clackety-clack* of the open car being drawn to the roller coaster's summit would soon be followed by riders' shrieks as their cars plummeted downward at speeds that felt like so many "Gs," even though the popular use of such gravitational concepts lay decades into the future.

Even after Parks Commissioner Robert Moses persuaded Mayor LaGuardia to give him jurisdiction of the Boardwalk and the beach in 1938, which allowed him to dampen some of Coney's ballyhoo, barkers' shouts continued to cajole eager crowds to try a tunnel of love here, a game of chance there. It was on June 16, 1884, that LaMarcus A. Thompson, rich from inventing seamless hosiery, opened the world's first roller coaster, his Switchback

Judging from the number of cars parked outside, Villepigue's Restaurant in Sheepshead Bay was still a favorite in the early days of the motor car among those who relished a trip to the ocean and a shore dinner to top it off.

City Parks Commissioner Robert Moses was all for rules and regulations. His beachfront prohibitions, in their own way, were almost as onerous as Prohibition, repealed shortly before LaGuardia appointed him to the post.

Railway, on West Tenth Street. Regrettably, it took decades for his Coney Island colleagues to recognize his accomplishment formally with a plaque: ". . . a Memorial to LaMarcus A. Thompson, the inventor of gravity"!

The popularity of Thompson's rig attracted other examples of the latest in amusement contrivances: the Thunderbolt, the Tornado, the Comet, the Rocket, the Giant Coaster, the Mile Sky Chaser, and, in 1927, the Cyclone, whose 100-second ride up and down nine hills is still considered one of the best in the world. Miniature airplanes tethered to revolving masts flew in tight circles, while the now-historic Loop-the-Loop seemed to defy the very gravity that Thompson was credited with inventing.

More traditional rides moved in sedate circles, horizontally or vertically. Carousels, featuring wild wooden steeds by Brooklyn master carvers like Marcus Charles Ilions and Charles Carmel, revolved to the hurdy-gurdy music of mechanical bands. The 250-foot-diameter Ferris wheel, introduced in 1893 at the World's Columbian Exposition in Chicago, never made it to Brooklyn, despite what newspaper clippings may say, but the 135-foot-diameter Wonder Wheel did, erected at its present location by Herman J. Garms, Sr., in 1920. What this variation on the original Ferris design lacked in size, capacity, and engineering sophistication, inventor Charles Herman's ride made up for in tricks. Passengers seated themselves in ranks in the Wonder Wheel's two dozen brightly painted metal-mesh cars that swung gently from the wheel's rim. Those who chose any of the sixteen colored ones thrilled when their car excitingly and unpredictably detached itself from the wheel's perimeter and took a shortcut to a position closer to its center, only to roll with increasing speed out to the opposite rim, seemingly propelling both car and passengers into space over the midway. Traditionalists learned to choose the white cars—they made the trip demurely along the wheel's entire circumference.

The range of rides in Coney's between-the-wars period was broad. For the bump-against-the-girl set, there was still Henry Elmer Riehl's ride, the Virginia Reel (a play on his daughter's name, Virginia Luna Riehl), introduced in the first decade of the century. Passengers sat in circular cars that revolved irregularly as they spun their way through a sloping, stunningly unconvincing painted landscape. (Riehl had earlier supervised construction of nearby Luna Park, which bore his daughter's middle name.) Less passive were the drive-them-yourself Dodgem cars, for mildly sadomasochistic patrons. So innocent while at rest, the cars began to buzz furiously once the power switch was thrown by the teen-aged ticket-taker with the inevitable acne. With all rules thrown to the winds, it was a case of "anything goes." The gyrations and impacts were further enlivened by the blue flashes of light arcing overhead in the dimly lit room when a car's copper contact shoe parted from the electrified wire-mesh ceiling with each collision. (The air had that special tang of ozone given off when a faulty light switch blew a fuse.) For the nautically inclined, there was a floating version of Dodgem, using electrically propelled miniature motorboats, also deriving power from an electrically charged overhead mesh. "Remember. Don't put your hands in the water!"

Where else but at Coney Island could all of this be matched by Dr. Martin Arthur Couney's Premature Baby Incubators? Moving from one Coney Island site to another between 1903 and 1943, often one step ahead of his detractors in the medical profession, Couney's sideshow attraction, featuring live premature infants, charged admission to see what he had begun in Germany as a *Kinderbrutanstalt*, a "child hatchery." (No wonder he emigrated.) Couney, a licensed physician, was actually very serious about his responsibilities, and though he harbored no illusions about the midway atmosphere, he charged his protégés' parents nothing for their children's care and came eventually to be widely respected by the medical community.

Despite Robert Moses' maxims, the beach could be lots of fun, as this scene shows, recorded by a Kodak Brownie. Knitting needles, in the bag in the foreground, never made the Parks Commissioner's list of the forbidden.

Every one of Coney Island's streets, alleys, and recesses that was zoned for amusement purposes—between West Fifth and West Nineteenth streets—offered fun-filled opportunities to satisfy most legitimate impulses. The most comprehensive array of all was behind the walls of George C. Tilyou's Steeplechase Park, between the Boardwalk and Surf Avenue on a large site that ran from West Sixteenth to West Nineteenth. STEEPLECHASE—THE FUNNY PLACE, the signs said, under an unforgettable face with a leering grin. Admission was charged at the gate, and everyone received a circular tag good for as many rides as there were numbers printed around its perimeter. For every ride taken, one of the numbers was punched until there were none. Always too soon.

Inside the gates lay a day's worth of fun and diversion, not unlike today's Great Adventure or the other theme parks that have recently gained favor—now that they can be built for accessibility by car, far beyond the reach of mass transit, and can charge fifteen-dollar admission fees.

Steeplechase's name derived from the ride on very visible, life-size, mechanical racehorses that sped along overhead undulating steel tracks that threaded their way through the park's grounds and into its handsome, white-painted, glass-enclosed Pavilion of Fun. The saddles were large enough for a couple and, reversing positions they might have taken on a Harley-Davidson, the guy would ride behind the girl with his arms around her. For those descending from the ride, a surprise lay in store. At the end of the long, dark exit ramp were vents through which a jet of compressed air caught many an unsuspecting young lady by surprise, blowing her skirt up around her waist, much the same way that Marilyn Monroe's did in *The Seven Year Itch*. Except that at Steeplechase there was always a large crowd waiting in the darkness beyond, who were willing to have their tickets punched one extra time to capture a glimpse of scanty underthings or catch a girl's scream of embarrassed surprise.

Other treats included a swimming pool, a small Ferris wheel, a merry-go-round, a rolling drum that you tried to circumnavigate without taking an unexpected spill, and the Human Whirlpool and the Chair-O-Plane, two attractions that Reginald Marsh immortalized in one of his many paintings of the Coney Island scene.

In 1941 the proprietors of Steeplechase re-erected the 250-foot-high Life Savers Corporation Parachute Tower—everyone called it the Parachute Jump. Salvaged from the recently closed

New York World's Fair, it was placed on a site in the park adjacent to the Boardwalk, where it survives unused. Since it had received a great deal of publicity as the prototype of a training device for army paratroopers, it became a very popular attraction during the early days of World War II, as it had been at the Fair. It was ballyhooed as offering the excitement of bailing out of a plane, without hazard or discomfort. As tame as the ride was in comparison with the real thing, it did offer the initial free-fall sensation and the gut-jangling jerk of the parachute billowing open, enough—perhaps more than enough—for most of its passengers, at least judging from the shrill squeals of its riders. The din emanating from the Parachute Jump, the roller coasters, and other reckless rides meshed with the piercing dissonances of BMT trains slowly curving into the Stillwell Avenue depot. It was hard to tell which sounds were which.

After the 1939–40 New York World's Fair, the Life Savers' Parachute Ride was taken down and re-erected at Coney Island where it was imprecisely dubbed the Parachute *Jump.* It only *felt* as though you were jumping.

Sailors find themselves having a
good time as they tumble in one of
Steeplechase's revolving barrels in
1953. The amusement park was a
favorite with servicemen right up
to its demolition in 1965.

Today the Parachute Jump stands mute and rusting. The trains, once chocolate brown, are now mostly silver and sleek and graffiti-covered. But come summer, thrill-seekers' screams still mingle with the subway's shrieking steel wheels. There are just fewer of them.

The exhilarating ride for which Steeplechase Park was named. Four horses, often carrying more than one rider, departed every thirty seconds to circle the enormous, glass-enclosed Pavilion of Fun. (Smart riders knew the horse carrying the heaviest weight always won.) The scene is in 1939.

13
LET'S EAT OUT T'NIGHT

break in the routine was always sought, and eating out was one of those breaks. Where you went depended on where you came from, how much cash you had to spare, and sometimes whether you had an excuse for getting away from Momma's kitchen. Eating out could be justified simply by an urge to go out. It might be a family tradition, like Sunday dinner, or a special event, like getting a raise, and might consist of a part of a day at Coney Island with a meal at Feltman's or Nathan's. A key factor was usually cost. Most of Brooklyn just wasn't affluent, and the many who needed to spread their bucks thin forced Brooklyn's eateries to offer flavorful cooking at a modest price. People with strong ethnic ties would often patronize only places with familiar cuisine. A notable exception was the Chinese restaurant. With so few Chinese living in Brooklyn, the chow mein/chop suey joints would never have survived without non-Chinese patronage. But for the rest, Italians went mostly to Italian restaurants, Germans to German, Near Eastern people to Atlantic Avenue, and Jews to neighborhood delicatessens or to kosher restaurants, like Rothman's on Kingston Avenue, or the Famous Dairy on Eastern Parkway.

If you patronized a local Italian eatery, then chances were that one of your favorite dishes was what was then called "ah-*beetz*," that flat, round pie of tomatoes and "mootz-a-*rell*" cheese, which has since become the national fast-food favorite we now know as pizza. In those days the signs and menus spelled it "apizza" and it could be bought only as a full pie served at a table, in the back, at

The main dining room of the Leverich Towers Hotel, at Clark and Willow streets, in Brooklyn Heights. The crisp white table linens and potted palms created an extraspecial atmosphere for that extraspecial meal.

FELTMANS' Upper Veranda Service the Shore Dinner DeLuxe CONEY ISLAND

the end of the bar. Not every Italian restaurant served apizza, but you could always get a bowl of spaghetti and meatballs with medium (not too spicy) sauce. The way to tell if you were in a good place was to inspect the tables as you entered. If the local Catholic priest in his Roman collar could be spotted enjoying his food, you could be certain you'd enjoy yours. A restaurant that recalls those kinds of places today is Bamonte's, still unpretentiously doing business on Withers Street in Williamsburg. It doesn't serve pizza, but the spotless white kitchen in the back, open to full view, gives it a genuineness not easy to find these days—and the gentle whiffs of garlic that find their way from the ranges to the tables help too.

Garlic may, in fact, be the common gastronomic denominator for most of Brooklyn's ethnic cuisines; it was certainly the mainstay of Brooklyn's many kosher delicatessens of that era, whose idiosyncratic aroma, derived from a liberal use of garlic in their cold cuts, announced their location at twenty paces, and whose sidewalks had a translucence that could be attributed only to regular—if unintentional—saturation with well-rendered chicken fat. (How Manhattan's few remaining midtown delicatessen-restaurants could ever have considered using burgundy-colored carpeting is hard to understand.)

Every neighborhood kosher deli in Brooklyn seemed cut from the same pattern; all had an appearance so easy to predict that their builders might have been observing an Eleventh Commandment. First, in the window, under the mandatory neon sign with Hebrew lettering and the brand of cold cuts sold, was the frankfurter grill, with ranks of red franks enjoying peaceful coexistence with rows of yellow knishes, a kind of potato patty. (Farther inside were "specials," what we today call knockwurst.) Adjacent were the obligatory mustard bowl and canister of steaming sauerkraut, awaiting the waiter's ritual summons, "Ordering two franks—with!"

Inside the door, you found a small, dark-stained, shiny wooden serving bar. Sometimes it even had a beer spigot and, to recall the character of a real bar, a short length of brass rail. And, of course, the cash register.

Next in line came the brilliant marketing ploy that must have been the first use of point-of-purchase merchandising: the sloped glass cases behind which lay delectable, tantalizing, mouth-watering displays of various kinds of cold cuts, all cut on the bias, the better to show their stuff. Hard salami, soft salami, chicken salami. Roast beef, rolled beef, corned beef. Bologna, brisket, tongue. (It wasn't until adulthood that I could allow myself to accept the fact that the tongue in the deli cases of my childhood was actually a cow's *tongue*.) No mortal could resist such temptations. Small wonder. Atop the meat case stood a teaser, an open display of small knobs of a thickly sliced *knublvoorsht*—garlic wurst—ornamented by a hand-lettered sign, A NICKEL A SHTICKL—a nickel apiece. They were the sachets of the delicatessen, redolent of garlic, and placed at adult nose level; gravity took care of us shorter kids. The owners really knew how to get your juices flowing.

Most people ordered sandwiches. The choice of breads was a limited one (remember, Henry Ford's Model T didn't offer many options, either): either rye, or what was called "club"—don't ask why—which was the deli's name for the crispy cuts of (forgive the expression) Italian bread.

Last in the ritualized row of glass cases came a taller one containing trays of cole slaw, potato salad, chopped liver, and small green cans of Heinz baked beans (not *pork* and beans, mind you) carrying the tiny symbol of anointment for those who cared, the encircled "U" of the Union of Orthodox Rabbis.

Everywhere embellishing the already overwhelming displays were, of course, the bulging multigallon jars of—shall we say—condiments. Who could call a meal in a deli complete without

The need to observe dietary laws hardly diminished the exuberant advertising at this kosher fast food emporium at 1711 Pitkin Avenue in Brownsville, photographed by Brooklyn chronicler N. Jay Jaffee in the 1950s.

these? Bottled sauerkraut, red peppers either sweet or hot, green tomatoes, and a variety of pickles ranging from really sour—wrinkled and olive-drab in color—to half-sour. These were plump, pimpled, still dark green, and almost white inside—the kosher pickle gourmet's delight.

Deli drinks, in those days before nondairy creamers, never included an option of coffee. It was tea (*mit* lemon) for the adults, served in a glass, and some kind of soda for the kids: Dr. Brown's cream or black cherry or ginger ale, or, for the grown-up seltzer drinker, Dr. Brown's Cel-Ray (celery) Tonic, the latter especially concocted to cut—psychologically, at least—through the deli's grease and garlic, and to restore good health and an Ipana breath.

Much of this is disappearing from our lives, and with it the subtlest of the deli's specialties, the tapers of mustard for take-out orders. Wrapped in little squares of buff-colored wax paper, these tiny cornucopias, deftly crafted in the deli's slow hours by the countermen, were what you took home to spread on your

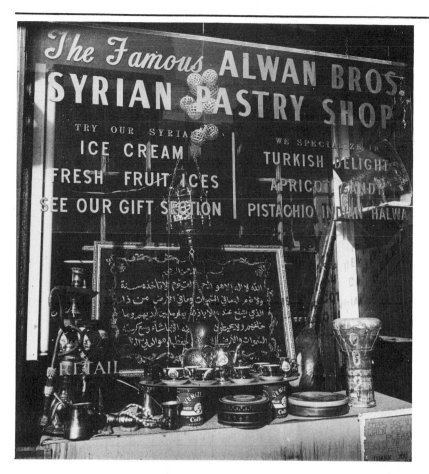

Arab restaurants and stores settled along Atlantic Avenue between Hicks and Court streets, particularly after lower Manhattan's middle eastern community was displaced from the Washington Street area by Robert Moses' Battery Park Tunnel.

bread when you ordered deli to go. Deli was cheaper that way, and loose cash was always hard to find. But nothing could taste as good as it did in the deli itself.

Garlic was a vital ingredient in Arab cooking, too. For those who lived in the vicinity of Atlantic Avenue, where the broad thoroughfare rose from the ferry slips, there was a good meal to be had in many a local Middle Eastern restaurant. The inexpensive meals, in those days reflecting the Lebanese and Syrian cuisines of the neighboring Arabic communities, often featured lamb purchased in kosher butcher shops. ("It's more tender there.") You could begin with an appetizer of hummous ba'tahini or the equally garlic-laced babaganouj, followed by kibbee, a ground lamb and pine-nut pie, or stuffed squash swimming in a sweet-sour yogurt soup. The menus featured many other special treats from the East (including something described as "foul mudammas," which revealed a failing in transliteration, not a self-critical review of the food).

Family dinners, one from column A and one from column B, were the staple of the traditional Cantonese Chinese restaurant menu. Meals began with "wanton of [*sic*] egg drop soup," followed by an egg roll, and topped off with kumquats and a complimentary fortune cookie.

In largely unconscious insult to the most populous nation in the world, eating Chinese food was always good-naturedly referred to by Brooklyn's predominantly non-Chinese population as "going to the Chinks." Eating out at the Chinks was sure to be economical. In those days the cuisine was Cantonese and *only* Cantonese, reflecting the origins of both owners and cooks (and everyone else Chinese). Steamed rice was the staple, fried rice the delicacy. After all, how much could a meal cost? Variety was encouraged through a formularized menu of two columns labeled A and B, respectively. The choice was invariably "one from column A, two from column B." What promptly came from the kitchen was al-

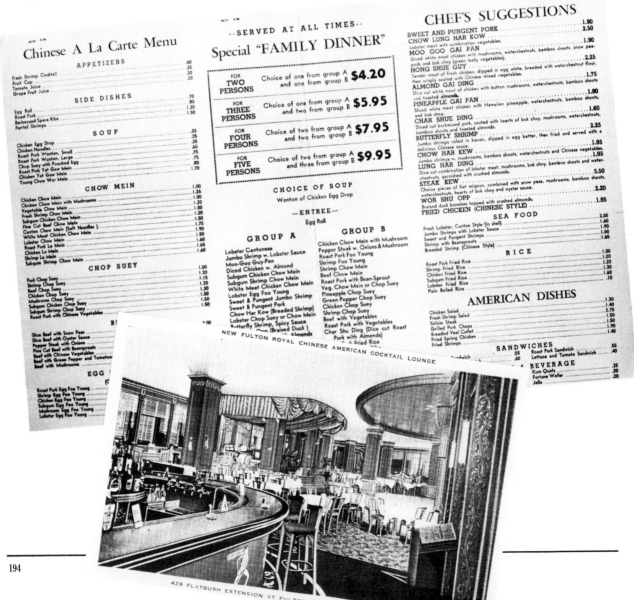

ways accompanied by a pair of tiny dishes of dark, thick duck sauce and hot mustard guaranteed to clear your nostrils better than Vick's VapoRub. Mysteriously labeled dishes like moo goo gai pan and subgum chow mein were tasted by all, since they were served family style in metal serving containers that faintly resembled a genie's lamp. Chinese meals couldn't help but be treats, particularly to the non-Chinese, which characterized at least 99 percent of the patrons. "Look, there are Chinese people eating here too, Pop—this must be a real good place!"

For many Brooklynites, the Chinese restaurant was the first step into that exotic world beyond Brooklyn into which their parents were struggling to gain them entry. Unlike other readily available restaurant choices—like Italian or Jewish or German—Chinese was associated with a people so remote and uncommon that it was, by simple examination, an automatically exotic cuisine. It was special (though bland and wholesome). It suggested the vastness of the earth in a way far more visceral than stamp-collecting ever could. It was so different that it offered those whose religious traditions seriously constrained their eating habits an easy excuse to leave their homes to taste the forbidden: beef with oyster sauce, lobster Cantonese, shrimp fried rice. "Hmmm. Not so bad, is it, Benny?"

Hearty seafood restaurants were also a tradition in Brooklyn. With all that coastline, thoughts of the sea's bounty could never be very far from a Brooklynite's mind.

Brooklyn's natural harbor for small boats, just a short troll from the Atlantic's waters, is Sheepshead Bay. To this day, that's where the freshest catch is available, and where the price may be haggled over on the still-briny deck of a day-fishing boat, just in from a sail.

To no one's surprise, therefore, Brooklyn's seafood restaurants tended to congregate nearby. Villepigue's Inn at Ocean and Voorhies avenues, almost at the door of the Sheepshead Bay Racetrack, served its first meal in 1886, the year the Gravesend track—the last of Brooklyn's three—opened. It remained in operation until after World War II, when it relocated to Times Square, where it joined a restaurant called McGuinness of Sheepshead Bay. Fresh fish were farther away, but customers were closer.

Nearer to the bay, on Emmons Avenue between East Twenty-sixth and East Twenty-seventh, was Tappen's, founded in 1845

by Jeremiah Tappan—the spelling changed at some point—a ho-
telkeeper from Grand Street in Manhattan. The restaurant stayed
in the family for over a century, until it was sold to Lundy's, down
the avenue, in 1948. Two years later the charming and venerable
eatery burned down and the name was sold to another restaurant
at Ocean Avenue and the Belt Parkway.

As evocative as these two seafood houses were, with all their
historicity and famous guests—like Lillie Langtry and Leonard
Jerome and the Goulds, Mackays, and Vanderbilts, the seafood
house that means much more to this period of Brooklyn history
was F.W.I.L. Lundy Brothers Restaurant, whose block-long, two-
story-high, mission-style structure still stands—unused today—
at the commanding site of Emmons and Ocean avenues.

Lundy's moved to its distinctive beige stucco-and-Spanish-tile
building in the mid-thirties, from its earlier site on a pier that jutted
into Sheepshead Bay's waters on Emmons Avenue's south side.
At its new location it had 2,800 seats and boasted that on a typical
Mother's Day it served ten thousand meals, and up to fifteen
thousand on other special occasions. Just poking one's head in
Lundy's door on any busy evening would lend credence to the
assertions. Before the aroma of the shore dinners could be assim-
ilated, the roar of thousands of conversations all but pushed the
new arrival back onto the avenue. Atmospheric, stuccoed, and
with lots of deep-red tiled floors everywhere, the interior guaranteed a ricochet of sound in every direction.

Once inside, one was quickly marched to a table, sometimes
out in left field, in an area no more unfamiliar to the guests, you
discovered, than to the waiters and busboys, who seemed not yet
to have found it. The wait for service approached the interminable,
though it was worth it. The menus were elaborate, detailed,
mouth-watering, and, after a period that allowed them barely to
be skimmed, were retrieved by the waiter, who would then call
you to attention and impatiently demand your orders, to be
shouted over the din.

Only then did the food begin to arrive, steaming hot, generous
in portions, and very, very fresh. It was worth it all. That's why
everyone came back for more. Lundy's was an American business
success story except for its labor problems, threats of shutdowns,
internal family disagreements, and finally a closing of its doors that
has left the place dark since 1979.

Inland from Brooklyn's shores, seafood could also be had, but

in combination with a wider range of dishes. Gage & Tollner's, still on Fulton Street, is considered by many to be one of Brooklyn's premier restaurants. Surely its decor, officially recognized by the city as both an exterior and interior landmark, is matched by none other, and the range of its menu recalls the excesses of Diamond Jim Brady and Lillian Russell. Michel's, at 346 Flatbush Avenue, close to Grand Army Plaza, was a standby since 1910, but couldn't hold out until Park Slope's gentrification was sufficiently under way. Peter Luger's, at Broadway and Driggs Avenue, started inauspiciously in 1876 as Charles Luger's Cafe, Billiards, and Bowling Alley. For years it was run by Charles's son Peter, called the "Beethoven of Beef." When he died in 1941, another son, Frederick, carried on. By 1950, however, the place had closed; auctioned off, it reopened and now survives as a steak establishment whose increased popularity threatens its character.

Ever hear about Joe's Restaurant? Which one? The one on Fulton Street? On Nevins? Joe's Seafood Inn along Sheepshead Bay? Or the one on Coney Island's Bowery? Each "Joe's" was cynically aware of the public's frail memory and therefore each contending for the title "original." Fulton Joe's, at the southwest corner of Pierrepont, though not the earliest, was the one that really generated the reputation enjoyed by all. Opened by Joe Balzarini on the "lower Fulton Street" site in 1909, it proved a success, catering to downtown businessmen, and by 1920 it had expanded its dining room into eight adjoining buildings, five on Fulton and three around the corner. In 1937, two years after Joe's

"F.W.I.L. Lundy Bros." said the sign facing Emmons Avenue in Sheepshead Bay. No one ever figured out the connection between the Mission style building, of beige stucco and Spanish tile, and the vast quantities of seafood served within, but the combination gave Lundy's an unforgettable image, nonetheless.

Joe's Restaurant, at Fulton and Pierrepont streets, was a downtown Brooklyn tradition for just short of a half century, closing in 1958. The restaurant rambled on and on much as the menu did. Many wondered how the chef did it.

death and after ten weeks of squabbling with their help, the owners sold the restaurant to their employees, who continued to run it successfully well into the fifties, when urban renewal of the Civic Center doomed the business. The last dinner was served on Christmas Eve of 1958, and within a month, an auction had disposed of all the fixtures but the bar, which had been purchased by the Mute Oxen Inn (a Catholic men's club) and removed to the old Crescent Club building a block away, today St. Ann's School.

To speak only of Brooklyn's restaurants would be to forget that Brooklynites patronized other kinds of eateries as well.

The fast pace of downtown's crowds made it a natural place for standup snack bars along Flatbush Avenue Extension and Fulton Street, which was then Brooklyn's entertainment crossroads. Alongside the penny arcades were open-fronted stands selling frankfurters, which could be washed down with a watered-down orange drink or more exotic beverages like papaya nectar, piña colada (without the rum), and coconut champagne; the stands resembled others that you could find in Times Square, Yorkville, or Coney Island. Less easy to forget were the chains (or the ones

that wanted to look like big chain operations, such as Uwanna, the Uneeda Biscuit of the frankfurter-stand circuit). More conscious of their corporate identity—and more sagacious in their negotiation of leases—some of their names are still with us: Nedick's, with its white porcelain front and dark green script sign, made their franks and orange drink seem like a banquet. The only controversy lay in the pronunciation of the name—was it Need-ick's or Ned-ick's? Pronunciation rules didn't help; neither did the sullen countermen. Nedick's big competitor, but one that was much more genteel in its approach, was Chock Full O' Nuts, begun by Bushwick High School graduate Charles Black. With a spartan menu including nutted cheese sandwiches and dreamy brownies— "no, ma'am, we don't serve tea"—a concern for cleanliness, and an eye for a distinctive graphic image, Black created a large chain of handsomely designed and exquisitely crafted snack bars, a few of which were in downtown Brooklyn. You met the nicest people at Chock Full, on both sides of the counter, as a matter of fact. The counterwomen were invariably black and invariably polite. And they *always* made certain the coffee spoon was balanced neatly on the cup. (When Jackie Robinson retired from baseball, he was persuaded to become the chain's vice-president for personnel.)

For those who had little money but lots of time, Brooklyn's cafeterias were the answer, where you could shmooze for hours over a cup of coffee or a glass of tea. In 1940 there were eight

JOE'S RESTAURANT

Brooklyn's Famous Eating Place

326-334 Fulton Street, Brooklyn, New York

ONLY DINING PAVILION ON THE WATER AT SHEEPSHEAD

DINE and DANCE
Our Specialty
ITALIAN DINNERS

SHORE DINNER
$2.00 $2.00
Relishes
Choice of
Crab Meat, Clam or
Shrimp Cocktail
Clam Chowder or
Chicken Soup
Steamed Clams with Broth
and Butter Sauce
Half Lobster and
Half Broiled Spring Chicken
Fresh Vegetables in Season
Home Made Pie or Ice Cream
Coffee, Tea or Milk

JOE'S SEA FOOD INN, 3000 EMMONS AVE., SHEEPSHEAD BAY

Bickford's cafeterias in Brooklyn, but none could compare with the Fulton Street Horn & Hardart Automat (of Children's Hour fame) where nickels (for the dispensing devices) were king, and the cashiers rarely miscalculated when they threw them out by hand across the dished marble counter of the change booth. Although the Automat did offer a novel mechanical food-dispensing system, baked macaroni in unique elliptical dishes, and dragon-shaped coffee spouts, it and the Bickford's units were still both chain operations, with food programmed by formula, and therefore all-purpose and bland. Offering considerably more character (in both food and clientele) were local operations like Garfield's ("the cafeteria of refinement") on Flatbush Avenue, at number 881, just above Church, or the two Dubrow's, one on Kings Highway and East Sixteenth and one on Utica Avenue (whose sign and Miami Beach Moderne bow front still can be seen at number 292). Hoffman's Cafeterias, of which there were three in Brooklyn, were on Flatbush, Brighton Beach, and Pitkin avenues. The latter, in the heart of Brownsville, never failed to attract its share of older, somewhat leathery, former ladies of the night drawn from the local community, together with a share of equally leathery lotharios still seeking favors.

Each of these cafeterias had similar characteristics. You pulled a ticket from a machine as you entered *(Gonnnng!)* and with each dish you purchased, your ticket was cumulatively punched, resulting in a total that you later paid on your way out. From the management's point of view, there were two problems. The schmoozers who kept too many chairs occupied for too long over a minimum purchase, and the freeloaders, who quenched their thirst with water, used the toilets, but ordered nothing. Abundant hand-lettered announcements threatened the latter with cafeteria-scaled cover charges for the return of an unpunched check. No one took the signs seriously.

The food was ordinary, although there were always a few complainers—very loud—and a few self-styled gourmands who swore the creamed spinach was spectacular—also very loud. Aside from the food, however, Brooklyn's cafeterias were certainly attuned to other needs of the proletariat. Tales of the Russian Revolution, for example, were counted and recounted.

Still, Brooklyn offered a number of elegant places to dine. Most of these were connected with the hotels in Brooklyn Heights, the borough's most urbane community and surely one of its most desirable, at least to those who were welcome. (A 1936 notice in

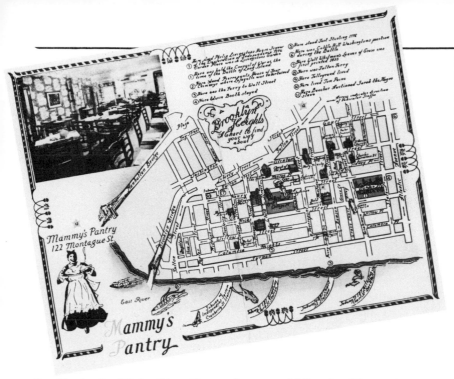

Montague Street's Mammy's Pantry offered visitors a folding postcard which doubled as a guided tour to Brooklyn Heights.

the *Eagle,* for Hicks Street's newly opened Mansion House Apartments, read, "Many long-term leases have already been signed with careful restriction of tenancy. . . .")

On Montague and Henry streets there were little restaurants, like Mammy's Pantry, which served Southern fare, such as Chesapeake Bay oysters as well as swizzles and juleps. At Yaffa's Drug Store at Clark and Henry, the claim was "Brooklyn's most beautiful fountain." In a tearoom on Henry Street, an emigré from Newfoundland opened a place in the early thirties that was named for herself—Patricia Murphy's Candlelight Restaurant. By introducing a new menu, candlelight, and warm, succulent popovers, she established a local culinary institution. By 1938 she had opened another outlet on Sixtieth Street in Manhattan, and the rest is history. The Candlelight, continuing to serve popovers but minus the Murphy name, remained a Heights favorite into the early sixties.

In those days the hotels on the Heights—the St. George, the Bossert, and the Leverich Towers—were considered pretty glamorous places to come to from all over the city, even the world. The Touraine Hotel, located on Clinton Street, close to the Fulton Street el, was off the beaten path. Attempts were made to "thoroughly overhaul" it in the early thirties, but it remained a lost cause and was finally demolished in '59.

While the Hotel Bossert, on Montague Street, was a dowager

ST. GEORGE
Natural Salt Water
SWIMMING POOL

The Most Luxurious in the World.

B15:— HOTEL ST. GEORGE, BROOKLYN, N. Y.

47784

CLOSE COVER BEFORE STRIKING

CLARK STREET, BROOKLYN, N.Y.

HOTEL ST. GEORGE

GREATER NEW YORK'S LARGEST HOTEL

GREAT NATURAL SALT WATER

POOL

dating from 1909, its Marine Roof, opened in 1916, offered smashing views of busy New York harbor that made it a very popular night spot of the twenties. It was outfitted like the deck of a luxury liner, complete with ships' bells, life preservers, and even a captain's bridge. Waiters were dressed as sailors, the maître d' like a ship's officer, and guests arrived in long dresses and tuxedos. Sundown brought a playing of Retreat by the orchestra, and as Old Glory was lowered, the staff stopped serving to salute the flag. Guests included movie stars like Pola Negri, politicians like Al Smith and Herbert Hoover, and media people like Briton Hadden and Henry Luce, who had recently founded *Time* magazine.

In the mid-thirties the Bossert provided the setting for the founding of a radio station. John Lawless Hogan, a well-known communications engineer, and Elliott M. Sanger, out of advertising and publishing, met there at dinner in 1935 to discuss converting the 250-watt amateur station W2XR into a commercial outlet with a focus on good music. The next year the agreement was in place and the name changed to WQXR.

The nearby St. George was even older than the Bossert, dating from 1885. Urged on by the Marine Roof's success, the St. George's owners decided to add a tall tower to their accretion of wings occupying most of a square block. The tower, completed in 1929, raised the hotel's total of rooms to 2,632, and allowed the St. George to label itself New York City's largest. It also added a roof restaurant sporting an elaborate lighting system called Color-

MARINE ROOF
HOTEL BOSSERT
MONTAGUE, HICKS AND REMSEN STREETS
BROOKLYN

ama, which allowed different moods to be achieved by the manipulation of twelve thousand colored lights. The roof's chief attraction, though, was its view. At night, to search out ships in the busy harbor, the hotel installed an enormous searchlight that remained active until 1932, when local residents, complaining of its glare, caused it to be removed. Thomas Wolfe's biographer, Andrew Turnbull, recounted a July Fourth sunset visit to the St. George Roof by the author in 1935, accompanied by his editor, Maxwell Perkins: "Looking across at the near-far splendor of Manhattan, gazing down on all the kingdoms of the world . . . Wolfe was filled with an ecstasy he had never known and would never know again."

An enormous illuminated sign stood atop the St. George, and was doubtless what impelled the Towers Hotel next door to apply in 1932 for a ten-foot-high sign of its own. Again, Heights neighbors balked, and the application for a permit was denied.

Down below, the hotel's owners, Bing & Bing, were in the process of building the St. George's most enduring and endearing contribution to Brooklyn's recent history—the mirrored fantasy of the St. George Pool. A $1.3-million saltwater creation that opened the next year, the pool featured decor by Willy Pogany, a popular artist of the time. It lured such celebrities as Buster Crabbe and Johnny Weissmuller to its 40 × 120-foot basin, and Eleanor Holm used its waters to rehearse the curvaceous swimmers for Billy Rose's Aquacade at the 1939 World's Fair. Most of all, it became a star attraction to innumerable Brooklynites over the many decades it was open.

14

DON'T TALK CHUM—
CHEW TOPPS GUM

T o those of us too young to be drafted or to work in the shipyards or to recognize how our pleasures would be rationed by government proclamation, World War II impinged only indirectly upon our lives.

First came the *Daily News*'s coarse, front-page halftones of Holland's peaceable windmills being devastated by the Nazi blitzkrieg. Then, a day or two after Pearl Harbor, the commander-in-chief's voice—"Presivelt" Roosevelt's, in some Brooklyn neighborhoods—crackled out of the table model, talking about that "day of infamy." How reassuring his voice was, filled with "calm certainty," so unlike Hitler's shrill rantings.

In those confused early days of the American involvement, Brooklyn quickly got its name into the war headlines. Capt. Colin P. Kelly, Jr., whose wife and son were staying with her folks in Brooklyn, was America's first World War II hero. It was his B-17 that was thought at first to have mortally wounded a Japanese battleship off the Philippines. His plane hit by enemy fire, Kelly ordered his crew to bail out, losing his own life when the damaged plane crashed. His bombardier, Sgt. Meyer Levin, of 1504 East Thirty-third Street in Brooklyn, got back to his base and became a local hero in his own right. In late 1942, to sell War Bonds, November 1st was declared Meyer Levin Day on his block, his parents proudly displaying his two awards, the Distinguished Flying Cross and the Silver Star. But war was no picnic. On January 7, 1943, Levin too was killed in action.

As the war proceeded, we paid more attention to Movietone

January 1, 1944, saw the launching of the USS *Missouri* down the Navy Yard ways into Wallabout Bay. The ship's greatest moment was when the Japanese signed the World War II surrender documents on her deck in Tokyo Bay the next year.

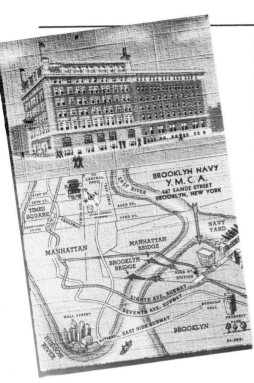

newsreels and "March of Time" specials showing those haunting black-and-white images of the *Lexington* and the *Saratoga,* defeated American aircraft carriers adrift in the Pacific. Their names ironically echoed those of the Revolutionary War battles—of more positive luster—that we'd been learning about in school. More and more, the Saturday-matinee "cowboy pictures" gave way to war films like *Bataan* and *Air Force* and *Action in the North Atlantic.* And in our mailboxes we started to receive miniatures from the boys overseas—"V-Mail" letters, flimsy and photographically reduced to save on bulk. Sometimes we were disappointed (but excited) to find that crucial portions had been blacked out by the censor to prevent critical information from falling into the wrong hands. (We all knew the slogan the borough's own chewing-gum manufacturer had coined: Don't Talk Chum—Chew Topps Gum.) Some of us even noticed anxious looks on the faces of adults. Were they a result of memories of the last war or were they fears of what might yet be in store in this one?

A few light moments even emerged before we were drawn into the fighting. Two lawyers about to forfeit a Brooklyn tenement for mortgage-payment default decided to convey the worthless property to Adolf Hitler and Joseph Stalin. The humorless bank, unable to find the new owners' addresses, sought them via ads in the local papers. The lenders eventually foreclosed, costing the lawyers $439.53 and a stern rebuke from an equally humorless judge.

Later, when the war was over and victory was ours, Borough President Cashmore tallied the grim statistics: some 327,000 men and women from Brooklyn had fought in the war; 7,000 of them had died in it.

To those who stayed home, there were the ration books, the OPA's price and wage controls, shortages, dimouts, and air-raid drills. Pleasure driving was out; those black-and-white "A" stickers on the windshield of the family car barely rationed enough gasoline to get it to the pump to buy more. Food rationing was divided between meat and dairy products (red tokens), and everything else (blue tokens). Victory gardens began in 1942 to help fill the vegetable gap, but even with the imposition of "meatless Tuesday," there simply wasn't very much meat or butter or eggs to go around. No wonder a 1945 raid on a Bath Beach residence netted twenty thousand counterfeit red stamps. We were enterprising to a fault.

The flashing incandescent and neon jangle of downtown Brooklyn's theater signs was extinguished, and all headlights were fitted with black "eyelids" once it was realized that the glow from the city's lights silhouetted convoys of troop and supply ships as they left the harbor, making them sitting ducks for the Führer's lurking U-boats.

At noon every Saturday, the city's innumerable air-raid sirens would wail in a test of their readiness. An ominous sound. Less frequently—and at night—men and women air-raid wardens, in overblown white tin hats that looked like World War I helmets with goiters, would conduct blackout drills. You had to be off the streets, and no lights were permitted indoors unless you had blackout curtains, which no one could afford. At times like those, Brooklyn felt like London.

So did the nights when antiaircraft searchlight beams traced paths across the threatening sky. Where did the beams come from, anyway? The feeling was like the newsreels from overseas, only there weren't any of those funny barrage balloons.

School windowpanes magically grew crisscrosses of translucent tape, and the fire drills that previously brought you downstairs to the street gave way to air-raid drills that marched you to interior corridors where you'd be safe from flying glass, if not necessarily from a direct hit. For the more drastic eventuality—though rarely mentioned—every school child was issued a little dogtag, a circular ivory plastic disk with name, birthdate, and address neatly engraved in blue by someone with a remarkably fine hand.

Brooklyn was hardly unfamiliar with the needs of the military. Since 1801, when the nation's first Navy Yard was established on the banks of Wallabout Bay, it had been a significant port of call for the United States Navy. The regular arrival of ships of the fleet was an important part of the local economy as well as a colorful activity in the streets abutting the Yard. Raucous bars, tattoo parlors, loose women, and cheap hotel rooms down Sands Street from the Naval YMCA beckoned thirsty, hungry, and frustrated sailors while offending proper folk.

Officers found Battleship Max Cohn's custom tailoring shop at 196 Sands Street a treasure. Many a naval officer, including Manila Bay's George Dewey and the South Pole's Richard E. Byrd, were fitted with spiffy dress uniforms there. The widely regarded skills of the city's garment workers helped fashion ordinary seamen's uniforms as well. Over at Third Avenue and Twenty-ninth Street, in two World War I loft buildings, 1,700 civil service seamsters and seamstresses sewed bellbottoms, jumpers, pea coats, and sailor hats for the navy's enlisted personnel.

The requirement that Navy brass purchase their own uniforms, the large number of officers passing through the Navy Yard, and Brooklyn's sizable pool of skilled garment workers made Battleship Max's a very popular institution along Sands Street in this 1938 view.

At the height of the Second World War, the Brooklyn Navy Yard was employing close to 71,000 workers on three shifts. Blue flashes from the arc welders' torches were visible day and night. With so many men off to the war, Rosie the Riveter became a Brooklyn fixture that came to symbolize—all too briefly—women's liberation from bondage at the kitchen sink.

While the Yard's enormous hammerhead crane, completed in 1939, just in time for the war, swung slowly to and fro, on the river itself the sleek shipbuilding ways were busy with the keels of battleships that would be outfitted there: the USS *North Carolina* in 1940, the USS *Iowa* in 1942, the USS *Missouri* in 1944. Brooklyn-built, too, would be the aircraft carriers *Bennington, Bonhomme Richard, Kearsarge*—and the *Franklin Delano Roosevelt,* launched in 1945 by the late president's widow.

Espionage was a great concern, and photography in the vicinity of the Navy Yard was prohibited by signs prominently displayed along its endless, forbidding walls. Similarly, photographs from the walkways of the East River bridges were also banned. Even so, everyone who used the bridges couldn't help but steal proud glimpses of the war effort being conducted in the Yard, hazy images that don't erase.

Not far from the Navy Yard, at the foot of the Manhattan Bridge on Flatbush Avenue Extension, the Sperry Gyroscope Company was fashioning those unerring devices that were to guide us to victory. Out in Red Hook, the Todd Shipyard Corporation was building funny little boats that turned out to be LCPs—Landing Craft, Personnel—which would one day deposit American troops on the beaches of Normandy and on the atolls of the South Pacific.

Southward along Brooklyn's shoreline, evidence of war was manifest. The navy occupied piers at Thirty-first and Thirty-third streets, while the army commandeered a group of six along Sheepshead Bay. Skirting Upper Bay between Fifty-eighth and Sixty-fifth streets was the Brooklyn Army Terminal, part of the New York Port of Embarkation, with its two enormously long, horizontal concrete structures whose sheer bulk rivaled the towers of today's World Trade Center. The terminal dispatched fully 50 percent of the East Coast's war-zone-bound cargo and sent off millions of American GIs on troop ships. Along the beach at Seagate, at Coney Island's western tip, evidence remains of concrete bunkers that held artillery aimed at the borough's sea approaches.

Farther out, at the eastern end of Manhattan Beach, where Kingsboro Community College now sits, the government pur-

chased 112 acres of privately owned land, on which it established the largest training stations for the coast guard and merchant marine. (It later turned out that fifty-two acres need not have been purchased at all; they were below the high-water mark and therefore government property in the first place.) In the same year the training stations were opened, 1942, Coney Island's Half Moon Hotel was requisitioned by the navy to become a convalescent hospital, later to be renamed Sea Gate after the nearby private community.

To protect this enormous concentration of wartime industrial and military activity, there was a largely invisible but equally immense behind-the-scenes military presence in Brooklyn. Atop roofs of structures around the Navy Yard, on the Squibb Building and nearby structures below Brooklyn Heights, along Imlay and Lorraine streets in Red Hook, and at Bush Terminal were installed elaborate emplacements of antiaircraft artillery, together with the

In the thirties, airplanes flying overhead were still a rare sight. Here, on September 22, 1938, a formation of U.S. Army Air Force B-18 bombers, experimental models later used for anti-submarine duty, cross the East River after passing over Brooklyn.

ammunition stores and troop barracks needed for the round-the-clock watch. Even Brooklyn's parks were not spared. Commandeered as sites for gun emplacements were Owl's Head Park, Liev (now Lief) Eriksson Square, Sunset Park, Dyker Beach Golf Course, and even pristine Prospect Park, where one of the most elaborate batteries of guns was established. It was only in March of 1944, when the facility was disbanded, that the army admitted what the Park Slope neighborhood had known for years. Some three hundred soldiers had staffed an extensive antiaircraft installation near Swan Lake that included cannon, underground ammunition dumps, observation towers, repair shops, and barracks. For years after the war had ended, evidence of the slit trenches and sandbagged gun sites continued to deface the park.

Brooklyn also harbored internment facilities. In Greenpoint there was an installation for Italian prisoners of war. Since the community had a sizable Italian population, there was a good deal of contact between locals and the POWs, with news from little villages in Italy making its way across the ocean, even though the war had effectively ended communication for some years. The neighbors brought food and hoped that their contact with these men would result in equally good treatment for their sons in Axis prison camps. A few of the contacts between the prisoners and the women of the community resulted in marriage after the war.

In May 1944, a temporary resettlement facility for formerly interned Japanese Americans was established at 168 Clinton Street in a Heights brownstone that had once been the Alpha Chi Rho fraternity house. The U.S. Army had decided that two and a half years of imprisonment were enough, and permitted some of the internees to resume civilian lives as best they could, even though the war was still on. The army offered inexpensive room

Antiaircraft installations dotted Brooklyn's parks and military bases during World War II. Here at Fort Hamilton following the Korean crisis, a 120 mm. AAA battery goes through its paces, in February 1953.

and board (a dollar a day, fifty cents for children) until a job materialized. Some sixteen hundred persons used the halfway house during the two years it was open.

As concerned as the authorities were with security matters during World War II, it was during a subsequent war, the Cold War, that Brooklyn and security became even more visibly linked. In December 1953, middle-aged and semiretired from photography, Emil R. Goldfus—bald, reticent, innocuous—left Manhattan's Upper West Side for the seedy edge of Brooklyn Heights. Apparently trying his hand at a new vocation, painting, he moved into a Hicks Street rooming house and rented a thirty-five-dollar-a-month space nearby at the obscure Ovington Studios Building, at 252 Fulton Street, designed by an equally obscure nineteenth-century architect, R. B. Eastman. The hulking, dark red structure was in its last days, awaiting demolition as part of the urban-renewal plan that was slowly rebuilding the Cadman Plaza area. A ground-floor tenant was a radio store where Goldfus would occasionally pick up a radio part or make some small talk with the owner. Upstairs, the Studio Building was a beehive of artists, poets, photographers, vocal instructors, even a greeting-card designer. Novelist Norman Mailer maintained a studio there. In the ensuing years, Goldfus developed a string of relationships with other tenants and their friends who have since made a mark in their respective fields. Among these were David Levine, now the acclaimed caricaturist, cartoonist Jules Feiffer, *Time* cover artist Danny Schwartz, Ralph Ginzburg—then an editor at *Look*—and painters Harvey Dinnerstein and Burt Silverman.

What a surprise for them—and for newspaper readers all over America—when they opened their afternoon papers on August 7, 1957, and read the headlines:

B'KLYN "ARTIST" UNMASKED
AS TOP SOVIET SPY IN U.S.
—*New York World-Telegram & Sun*

RED POSING AS B'KLYN ARTIST
INDICTED AS TOP SOVIET SPY
—*New York Journal American*

And the next morning:

INDICT SOVIET'S
U.S. SPY BOSS
—*New York Daily News*

NAB B'KLYN "ARTIST"
AS TOP SOVIET SPY
—*New York Mirror*

Could they mean the mild-mannered, guitar-playing, sinus-suffering Emil Goldfus? The generous, indulgent father figure who came to be accepted and regarded as a friend by his artist neighbors? The paintings that covered the walls of his studio bore witness to the three years he'd spent painting in Brooklyn. (David Levine still remembers Goldfus's love of Lorna Doone cookies; looking back, he wonders if they were intended to go with the unconvincing Scottish burr in Goldfus's speech.)

But Goldfus wasn't Goldfus, or Collins, or Kayotis, or Milton, or Mark—his other names; he was, in fact, Col. Rudolf Ivanovich Abel of the KGB, the Soviet State Security Service, "the highest-ranking espionage agent ever caught in the United States."

Colonel Abel was later tried in the old Federal Courthouse adjoining the Main Post Office, directly across the park from the Ovington building. Convicted, he was sentenced to prison. Some among those who'd gotten to know Abel continued to believe that the whole affair was just a bad dream, until early one winter morning in 1962, across a deserted bridge connecting West and East Germany, American prisoner Emil Goldfus–Rudolf Abel was traded to the Russians for a Russian prisoner, Francis Gary Powers, pilot of America's U-2 spy plane.

The afternoon papers carried the news of Hitler's May 8, 1945, defeat to these elated Bensonhurst residents displaying V-for-Victory signs, made famous by Winston Churchill.

15

YOU SHOULDA BEEN HERE WHEN...

emories of the place associated with one's childhood inevitably include those of losses—among others, literal loss of property and life, in catastrophes like storm or fire. Brooklyn had its share of such disasters.

The topsy-turvy disarray of concrete that was once Manhattan Beach's shorefront esplanade remains to this day an inadvertent memorial to the Atlantic's stormy fury. The scars of Brooklyn's fires, on the other hand, are less easy to identify, as immense as some of them were. Many of the worst infernos were concentrated along its shores.

The traditionally flimsy nature of amusement park construction, teamed with strong winds off the ocean and low water pressure, produced some of the most thrilling of Coney Island's spectacles—those cataclysms that resulted in the fiery loss of some of its great amusement attractions.

By the 1920s, such conflagrations had already established the impermanence of Coney's amusement parks. Only a decade old, Steeplechase Park burned in 1907, to be rebuilt the next year into its more famous, glassed-in version. The legendary Dreamland lasted only seven years, burning to the ground in 1911. Many other fires followed, like the one that began along the Boardwalk on the midsummer afternoon of July 13, 1932, leaving five thousand homeless and destroying the possessions that countless others had left in the burned bathhouses. With Coney so far from the city's watershed, water pressure out there was very low, far below the special needs of the fire department in time of peril.

The roller coaster, with the curious name *Mile Sky Chaser,* burns on Saturday, August 12, 1944—at the height of the summer season—in one of the many conflagrations suffered by Coney Island's Luna Park.

"Swept by Ocean Breezes" **Manhattan Beach Estates**

A pre-1920 promotional piece showed the Manhattan Beach Promenade filled with fashionable strollers. Over the years, wind, waves, and storms have tossed its concrete slabs around in a topsy-turvy way.

Onshore winds could often conspire to fan the flames. So in 1937 the city built a special high-pressure water system for the Coney Island amusement area, complete with its own modernistic pump house that made Neptune Avenue and West Twenty-third Street look as if it were part of the upcoming '39 World's Fair. But even with the added water pressure, Luna Park, Coney's other great amusement center, built in 1903, finally ran out of luck in 1949, when what little remained after the disastrous fire of 1944 and another in 1947 burned to the ground.

Closer to downtown were the Furman Street warehouses, lining the East River beneath the brow of Brooklyn Heights, stout brick edifices resembling those making up the Empire Stores, near Fulton Ferry. As handsome as the post–Civil War structures were, their inaccessibly large floor areas and lack of sprinklers, combined with their highly inflammable contents, made them the curse of the city's firefighters. This became evident one Saturday afternoon in the spring of 1935, when the contents of New York Dock Company Stores 38 and 39 began to burn in a spectacular eight-alarm blaze that continued out of control for days, until the floors and roof collapsed under the effects of flame and water. People on the Wall Street subway platform in Manhattan were felled by the billowing smoke that was sucked into the tunnels through the adjacent Furman Street ventilators of the IRT Seventh Avenue line. When the count was complete, 1,068 persons had been injured, and the taste of acrid smoke from smoldering crude rubber and rolls of tarpaper hung in the area for a long time.

On a cold winter afternoon in 1956, cargo stacked on the Luckenbach Steamship Pier, located at the foot of 35th Street in Gowanus Bay, then the longest pier in the city, exploded with a force that was felt six miles away. The ensuing fire, whose flames shot five hundred feet into the sky, resulted in a nine-alarm borough call that brought masses of firefighting equipment and an array of fireboats to the scene. Among the cargo that fueled the blaze were detonator caps and foam rubber. So intense was the heat that four neighboring piers caught fire. When the smoke cleared, ten persons were dead, more than 250 injured.

In Coney Island today, Dreamland's site is occupied by the pretentious building of the New York Aquarium, an institution sent into exile from Battery Park by Robert Moses. Luna Park became the site of banal high-rise housing. Furman Street's warehouses were demolished in the fifties, making it easier to view the Manhattan skyline from the Promenade and to see the Port Authority's newly built, flimsy-looking blue piers, whose usefulness in turn has recently ended. The Luckenbach Pier and its neighbors were replaced by the Northeast Marine Terminal, marked by a pair of giant birdlike cranes, emblematic of the coming of containerization to the Port of Brooklyn.

But what of those parts of Brooklyn's physical heritage that resisted fire and flood? Standing proudly at the brow of Brooklyn Heights, where it had looked over the harbor since 1889, was the Hotel Margaret, which caught fire in a pelting rain on the evening of November 23, 1923. Confined to the upper two floors, the eleventh and twelfth, the flames were visible across the river and to crowds of curious onlookers who filled the streets below, already clogged with fire apparatus. Two hundred guests and residents were evacuated, among them the acerbic Joseph Pennell, an outstanding printmaker and illustrator of his time, who complained bitterly about the fire department's failure to fight the fire in a timely and efficient manner. Luckily, the renowned art collection housed in his eighth-floor apartment was saved. But the Margaret was in the ranks of the doomed. Decades later, in the early-morning hours of February 1, 1980, it again caught fire, this time as it neared the completion of an extensive renovation. It was vacant. With no one to spread the alarm, the flames had a good head start. The near-zero temperatures and high winds, which left the streets picturesque with ice, hindered firefighting, and the end this time was truly final. Much of the newly renovated structure collapsed, and what remained was deemed unsafe and quickly demolished.

Sometimes losses more ephemeral than those from fire and

Two venerable brick warehouses along Furman Street containing tar paper and crude rubber caught fire on April 20, 1935, and burned out of control for days filling the area and even the nearby subway tunnel with acrid smoke.

SECTION OF ORCHESTRA & BALCONY MARK STRAND THEATRE. FULTON ST. AND ROCKWELL PL. BROOKLYN, N.Y.

storm can be even more deeply felt—as in the case of some of those that emerged after World War II.

The end of the war brought veterans home from service, and private cars back from forced retirement. Aided by federal mortgage guarantees, abetted by subsidized super highways, and seduced by the cute ranch houses and split-levels being built on the dreary potato fields of central Long Island and other open sites, young families were lured from Brooklyn and other inner-city areas into suburban living. New houses to live in, new places to shop, new schools for the children to attend.

They were leaving the old neighborhood, those kids you grew up with, the boys who served in Europe, North Africa, the South Pacific, or on Atlantic Patrol; the girls you met at the senior prom. All were seeking a better life out there, in Nassau County or Bergen or Westchester. Even older folks saw the possibilities of a better life across the line in Queens, in Kew Gardens Hills or Flushing, if not farther out on the Island, where their grown children had moved.

With these departures went part of Brooklyn's labor-skills pool. A signal began to flash to local manufacturers that a one-story factory in the suburbs made more sense than an upper-floor Brooklyn loft operation, dependent as it was upon a broken-down freight elevator and a broken-down operator to match. The growth of unions and the improvement of urban wages and working conditions gave other reasons for flight: lower wages and benefits, lower taxes, a smaller nut to crack to keep the business going. Some industries stayed, like brewing. But on April Fool's Day, 1949, the International Union of Brewery, Soft Drink, Cereal, Distillery, and Grain Workers of America struck the city's fourteen remaining breweries, idling seven thousand workers for eighty-

The first of 77th Division troops to be returned from Japan after the signing of the surrender on September 2, 1945, shown leaving Sapporo, Hokkaido, in October of that year.

one days, well into the warm months of May and June. It was the beginning of the end for most of Brooklyn's breweries, even though the last didn't close until 1976.

Even the Navy Yard, once New York State's single largest industrial facility, started to wind down following World War II. The big war was over and, even with the fighting in Korea, what large contracts remained were often going elsewhere. The Navy Yard finally closed in 1966.

Even before the war, the value of water-borne transportation began to fade. First it was the ferries. The old Fulton Ferry, which had held on long after the opening of the Brooklyn Bridge, made its last trip in 1924. The early thirties saw the demise of the Atlantic Avenue, Broadway, and Grand Street ferry routes across the river. By the end they served mostly people who lived at the

In June of 1940, the trek home from the downtown intersection of Flatbush and Nevins meant a trolley journey for the many, a cab ride for the few. The young fellow squatting over the subway grating is looking for a nickel to get him home, to be lifted from the darkness below by a wad of sticky chewing gum at the end of a string.

water's edge—poor people, and horsedrawn wagons whose tired steeds couldn't take the bridges' steep grades.

Trolley cars remained until after the war. But even they, so familiar, so deeply ingrained in Brooklyn's history, and responsible as they were for the naming of its ball team, began to disappear. As early as the twenties, "trackless trolleys" started to appear, those electric buses with a funny double set of wires overhead. Now, with the war's end, while helping to make the suburbs more accessible and easily negotiable, Detroit turned its attention to reworking the cities, as well. With the help of the oil and rubber interests, they turned their attention to ridding the nation's cities of vast trolley empires in favor of fossil-fueled, rubber-tired buses.

Brooklyn was one of their many successes. Brooklyn's trolleys began to be phased out in 1947, and the last, the lines along Church and McDonald avenues, began their final, mournful runs before dawn on October 31, 1956.

To the demographic, industrial, and transportation losses must be added the personal ones. Like those of sons, brothers, husbands who went off to war—to places never covered in geography class, like Luzon, St. Lo, Guadalcanal—and never came back, or did come back, but not whole. It didn't matter whether they were heroes, like Colin Kelly's bombardier over the Philippines, or that nice boy next door. Out of the corners of our eyes we noticed more and more little Gold Star pennants in front windows. Sometimes there was a quiet buzz among the neighbors, and the block was stilled for a time. Among devout Catholics—there seemed to be so many more then—black and purple bunting would then

Children at play in the summer of 1934 near a dilapidated frame house on Little Street in Vinegar Hill. It stood adjacent to the steel cage over the Navy Yard's shipbuilding ways, from which many warships were launched.

Their uniforms look a bit rumpled, but these servicemen had gone through a lot and it was good to have them home again. Crowds turned out in every neighborhood to welcome them back.

drape a house that had been touched. There would be wakes and tears.

As the tide of the war shifted and one looked toward its end, patriotic groups gathered at unused lots to solemnly dedicate name-filled war memorials—wooden billboards, really, but heart-felt tributes, nevertheless, to those who had gone and who wouldn't come back. When the pre-draft-age bugler sounded Taps, the eyes of even the most manly in the crowd brimmed.

And in time—too short a time—these memorials, too, were forgotten and disappeared.

It was only the gravestones in Brooklyn's cemeteries that provided permanent reminders of the toll of war and, of course, of life in general. Out on Jamaica Avenue there was the National Cemetery, Brooklyn's version of Arlington, whose crisp rows of crosses and occasional Stars of David marked off the rambling contours of neat green lawn, tended so carefully by the federal government. Greenwood, whose rich statuary offered an unrivaled index of nineteenth-century heroes and heroines to a totally uninterested citizenry, continued to accommodate Brooklyn's dead, but the monuments were more ordinary now, homely in comparison to their predecessors. As were those in cluttered Holy Cross and

The cruiser USS *Pensacola* is escorted to a dock after being launched at the Navy Yard on April 25, 1929. Judging by the large number of people who attended the ceremony, a launching was an important event, even in peacetime.

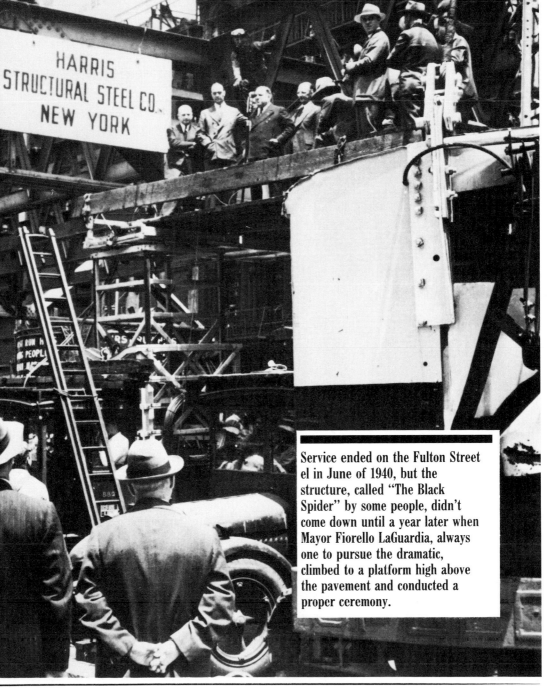

Service ended on the Fulton Street el in June of 1940, but the structure, called "The Black Spider" by some people, didn't come down until a year later when Mayor Fiorello LaGuardia, always one to pursue the dramatic, climbed to a platform high above the pavement and conducted a proper ceremony.

Washington cemeteries and Brooklyn's many others, where the
sons and daughters of the working class were laid to rest.

Whole parts of Brooklyn are gone now.

Downtown Brooklyn is a new place; the Civic Center is its new
name, or Fulton Mall. The Fulton Street el came down in 1941,
the year after service stopped. Built of pipe cleaners and bubble
gum, they used to say. Good riddance. Finally we can see sunlight.
But they've also taken actual parts of Fulton Street away. They
waited until the passage of Local Law 27 of 1967 to change its
name to Cadman Plaza West between Pierrepont Street and the
old ferry landing. But first they robbed us of a piece of historic
Fulton Street's very route. Our well-meaning planners almost to-

tally erased the curving part next to Borough Hall—for park use, they said. Parking for judges also turned out to be a "park" use. (To find Fulton Street's original path, look for the IRT subway gratings on the diagonal.)

With the el removed, it was puzzling that Fulton Street's big department stores, such as Namm's and Frederick Loeser's (pronounced "*Lo*-zhurs"), and the smaller ones, such as Oppenheim Collins, closed. Why didn't they flourish in the newly revealed daylight? Retailing and photosynthesis must not have very much in common. The departure of the el may have been a good thing, but the closing of those stores robbed downtown of even more of its special character.

And what about Fulton Street's theaters? On the other side of Flatbush Avenue, their presence is today barely noticeable on the dingy barren thoroughfare. Dancer Twyla Tharp recently considered reviving one of them to build upon the successes of nearby BAM, but live theater—later changed to burlesque—has been gone from Fulton Street for decades. And the movies *cum* stage shows at the Brooklyn Paramount (1928–1962) and Fabian's Fox (1928–1966) are gone as well.

The curious triangular site of the Fox, so perfectly suited for a twenties' motion picture palace, now accommodates Con Edison's handsome downtown headquarters—a victory for modern architecture, a defeat for downtown's vitality. A couple of blocks north, the Paramount's dun brick shell continues as Long Island University's Tristram W. Metcalfe Hall, which, back in 1950, LIU purchased with a long-term leaseback to Paramount. Not long

The sheer size of the Brooklyn Paramount Theatre, evident in this 1929 portrait, contributed enormously to Brooklyn's pride. The building at Flatbush Avenue Extension and DeKalb Avenue still stands as part of LIU's Brooklyn Campus, but its marquee and monumental neon signs are gone. Its once magnificent interior, by the same architect who designed Times Square's Paramount, is now the college's gymnasium.

enough; the once-lavish interior now serves as LIU's gymnasium, hardly an appropriate reuse for so evocative a neo-Baroque space. Although the mighty Wurlitzer is still there, it's brought up from the deep only for very special occasions. George Metesky, the "Mad Bomber," thought enough of the Paramount during the 1956 Christmas season to deposit one of his explosives among its 4,188 seats. (That blast reopened the decades-old case and led to his capture the next year.) The structure remains, but where are the thousands who converged on it to see the Paramount's Hollywood spectaculars and the accompanying stage shows—or those who more recently waited hours on line to see Murray the K's rock-'n'-roll extravaganzas?

Beginning in the mid-fifties, the Victorian legacy surrounding Borough Hall finally began to tumble down after almost a half-century of proposals for making Brooklyn's office area a "city beautiful." With no protection from a municipal landmarks commission, almost everything in sight turned to dust, the unworthy along with the worthy. The Arbuckle Building, the Jefferson Building, the Hall of Records, the old Kings County Courthouse with its funky egg-shaped dome, all came down and the geography of the Borough Hall area was almost entirely reworked.

Among the buildings slated for demolition in the Borough Hall area was the Eagle Building, across Johnson Street from the Main Post Office. A new, modern printing plant was nearing completion nearby, but as it turned out, Brooklyn's own newspaper unexpectedly folded before its building did. The last edition of the 114-year-old *Eagle* rolled off the presses on January 28, 1955. And with it ended an institution that had contributed mightily to Brooklyn's sense of self. The City of Brooklyn may have been absorbed into the City of New York in 1898, but at least its name continued to be carried proudly, seven days a week, on the front page of the *Eagle*. With that journal's demise, Brooklyn lost yet another important vestige of its identity.

The ornate bronze torcheres that guarded the steps of the old Kings County Court House frame a view of Borough Hall and the Court Street skyscrapers beyond, on a mid-fifties spring afternoon.

There have always been those who saw Brooklyn as a "banana republic" open for colonialist exploitation. Robert Moses was such a person. To Moses, Brooklyn's greatest value was as a land bank for his schemes. In 1938 he proposed—in implementation of the Gowanus Parkway section of the city's circumferential highway, Belt Parkway—a ninety-four-foot-wide road atop the pillars of the discontinued BMT Third Avenue el, which had formerly bathed only forty feet of that shopping street in what Moses' biographer, Robert Caro, calls "a Venetian-blind shadow." Moses' overhead "parkway" killed Third Avenue, and its effects on adjacent Sunset Park are still evident. Brooklyn's next role was as anchor for Moses' scheme for a Battery-Brooklyn Bridge. (Yes, a bridge!) That destructive idea would certainly have defaced the Lower Manhattan skyline. While his enemies won a victory on that one, Moses punished them by cynically using the old Dreamland site in Coney Island as a dumping ground for the New York Aquarium, which he had banished from Battery Park. On the other hand, when Moses saw something in Brooklyn he liked, he tried to ease it out to Manhattan. Case in point: the handsome equestrian statue of General Grant in Grant Square. Twice (in 1938 and 1941) he tried to have it relocated at Manhattan's Grant's Tomb; twice he lost. It still stands at Bedford and Rogers avenues.

Sometimes Moses also gave, but not without a fight. The Brooklyn Heights Promenade was a Moses venture, but one that he was pressed into supporting only after giving up his plan to carry the Brooklyn-Queens Expressway through the Heights in a block-wide gash along Hicks Street, the route it takes through Cobble Hill, to the south. As his Gowanus Parkway killed Third Avenue, this would have killed the Heights. As it is, construction of the Promenade wiped out a charming nineteenth-century fixture anyway—architect Minard Lefever's Penny Bridge over Montague Street, connecting Pierrepont Place with Montague Terrace.

At one point, clever politicians even tried to make off with another of Brooklyn's bridges, this one among her proudest possessions, the Brooklyn Bridge. MUST TEAR DOWN BROOKLYN BRIDGE TO REBUILD IT, screamed the front-page *Brooklyn Eagle* headline on July 30, 1922. City Commissioner of Plants and Structures Grover Whelan had announced he was planning to scrap what his engineers had termed "an unsafe structure" down to the foundation of its historic towers. When a reporter asked to interview his engineers, Whelan said, "I cannot do that . . . all the engineers could tell you in addition to my own statement would be technical details which the public would not understand." As a reward for his characteristic candor, Whelan was later appointed police commissioner by Mayor Jimmy Walker, and eventually, director of the money-losing 1939 World's Fair. It later turned out that Whelan's bridge heroics were intended as scare tactics. He had already closed the bridge to traffic a few days earlier when he claimed a cable had slipped. Actually, a $50-million proposal to build another East River crossing north of the Williamsburg Bridge was before the Board of Estimate, and there was some concern—well taken, it would seem—that the scheme wouldn't make it without a bit of public massage. It didn't work.

Brooklyn had lost many of its institutions during this era, and important pieces of its urban fabric, too. Old social clubs like the Hamilton, the Crescent, the Midwood, and the Germania had disappeared. The Dodgers had opted for the Los Angeles smog. But Brooklyn's most important loss in this period was a loss of confidence. Between 1950 and 1957 alone, Brooklyn lost a total of 135,000 men, women, and children. They were buying the blarney about the suburbs, they were buying cars, they were moving out to the sticks. Filling the housing vacuum they left behind, 100,000 newcomers moved in, many of them black and Puerto Rican, many also seeking a better tomorrow, as their predecessors had. Another wave of resettlement for Brooklyn. But rich resources unique to Brooklyn were forgotten. And many of the borough's sons and daughters had been dispersed across the breadth of the land, one day to think back on how life had once been in Brooklyn.

16

LEND ME YA CAR!

ey, Lenny."

"Yeah."

"Lend me ya car?"

"What for?"

"Me and Francine wanna go out to Levittown to see her cousin. She says it's terrific out there for the kids, and we wanna see for ourselves. So, what d'ya say?"

"Uh . . . I dunno, Vince. I was thinking of taking a ride out to Jones Beach."

"Ah, come on, Lenny. How about it?"

"Listen, Vince. Don't ya think it's about time you got a car of your own?

"Yeah . . . maybe so . . . maybe I should."

And for a lot of us, that's how Brooklyn ended.

In the decades that followed World War II sinuous ribbons of concrete, such as the Southern State Parkway here shown near Malverne, Long Island, lured young Brooklynites to explore—and then colonize—the nearby suburbs.

PICTURE CREDITS

The author gratefully acknowledges the use of photographs and memorabilia from the following sources. Photographs not listed here are from the author's private collection or in the public domain.

Every effort has been made to trace the proper copyright holders of the photographs used herein. If there are any omissions we apologize and will be pleased to make the appropriate acknowledgments in any future printings.

BIBLIOGRAPHY

GENERAL

Agee, James. "Brooklyn is . . . one corner of a foreign field that is forever Flatbush." *Esquire,* December 1968.

Bird, Robert S. "Whatever Happened to Brooklyn?" *The New York Herald Tribune,* February 15–21, 1962.

Brenner, Anita. "A Borough, a City, Another World—Brooklyn." *The New York Times Magazine,* January 22, 1939.

Brooklyn Chamber of Commerce. *Brooklyn, the Greatest Borough of the Greatest City in the World.* New York, 1923.

———. *Brooklyn, New York City.* Brooklyn, 1928.

The Brooklyn Daily Eagle. *Eagle Almanac.* Brooklyn, 1920–29.

City of New York. *Official Book of the Silver Jubilee of Greater New York.* New York, 1923.

Civic Council of Brooklyn. *Ten Years of Progress.* Brooklyn, 1933.

Community Council of Greater New York: Bureau of Statistical Services. *Brooklyn Communities: Population Characteristics and Neighborhood Social Resources.* 2 vols. New York, 1959.

Consolidated Edison Company of New York. *The Population of New York City by Districts, 1910–1948.* New York, 1948.

Hamill, Pete. "Why I Live in Brooklyn." Reprinted in *The New York Daily News,* May 2, 1979.

Latimer, Margaret. *Brooklyn Almanac: Illustrations/Facts/Figures.* Brooklyn: The Brooklyn Educational & Cultural Alliance, 1984.

Liben, Meyer. *New York Street Games.* New York: Schocken Books, Inc., 1984.

McCullough, David W. *Brooklyn . . . and How It Got That Way.* New York: The Dial Press, 1983.

Miller, Ruth Seiden, ed. *Brooklyn U.S.A.* Brooklyn: Brooklyn College Press, 1979.

Murphy, Mary Ellen, Mark Murphy, and Ralph Foster Weld, eds. *A Treasury of Brooklyn.* New York: William Sloane Associates, Inc., 1949.

Philips, McCandlish. *City Notebook: A Reporter's Portrait of a Vanishing New York.* New York: Liveright Publishing Co., 1974.

Richmond, John, and Abril Lamarque. *Brooklyn, U.S.A.* New York: Creative Age Press, 1946.

Schoenbaum, Eleanora W. "The Emergence of Brooklyn's Fringe Areas 1850–1930." Ph.D. diss., Columbia University, 1976.

Wexelstein, Leon. *Building Up Greater Brooklyn.* Brooklyn, 1925.

White, Norval, and Elliot Willensky. *The A.I.A. Guide to New York City.* New York: Macmillan Publishing Co., 1967, 1968, 1978.

Works Progress Administration. *New York City Guide.* New York: Guild's Committee for Federal Writers' Publications, Inc., Random House, 1939.

COMMERCE AND INDUSTRY

Anderson, Will. *The Breweries of Brooklyn.* Croton Falls, N.Y., the author, 1976.

Boyd, Brendan C., and Fred C. Harris. *The Great American Baseball Card Flipping, Trading, and Bubble Gum Book.* Boston: Little, Brown and Co., 1973.

Bunker, John G. *Harbor & Haven.* Woodland Hills, Cal.: Windsor Publications, Inc., 1979.

Filipetti, George. *The Wholesale Markets in New York and Its Environs.* Regional Plan of New York and Its Environs, Economic and Industrial Survey. New York: The Regional Plan Association, 1925.

"A Final Tribute to the New York Naval Shipyard, 1637, 1801, 1966." *All Hands,* December 1966.

Fried, Frederick and Mary. *America's Forgotten Folk Arts.* New York: Pantheon Books, 1978.

Hendrickson, Robert. *The Grand Emporiums: The Illustrated History of America's Great Department Stores.* Briarcliff Manor, N.Y.: Stein and Day, 1979.

Mangels, William F. *The Outdoor Amusement Industry from Earliest Times to Present.* New York: Vantage Press, Inc., 1952.

Schroth, Raymond A., S.J., *The Eagle and Brooklyn: A Community Newspaper 1841–1953.* Westport, Conn.: Greenwood Press, 1974.

Tuleja, Thaddeus V. "A Short History of the New York Navy Yard." Typescript pamphlet at Long Island Historical Society. Brooklyn, 1959.

West, James H. "A Short History of the New York Navy Yard." Typescript pamphlet at Long Island Historical Society. Brooklyn, 1941.

CRIME

Arm, Walter. *Pay-Off: The Inside Story on Big City Corruption.* New York: Appleton-Century-Crofts, Inc., 1951.

Bernikow, Louise. *Abel.* New York: Trident Press, 1970.

Fried, Albert. *The Rise and Fall of the Jewish Gangster in America.* New York: Holt Rinehart and Winston, 1980.

Gosch, Martin A., and Richard Hammer. *The Last Testament of Lucky Luciano.* Boston: Little, Brown and Co., 1975.

Joselit, Jenna Weissman. *Our Gang. Jewish Crime and the Jewish Community 1900–1940.* Bloomington: Indiana University Press, 1983.

Lee, Henry. *How Dry We Were: Prohibition Revisited.* Englewood Cliffs, N.J.: Prentice-Hall, Inc., 1963.

Peterson, Virgil W. *The Mob.* Ottowa, Illinois: Green Hill Publishers, Inc., 1983.

THE DODGERS

Durant, John. *The Dodgers: An Illustrated Story of Those Unpredictable Bums.* New York: Hastings House, 1948.

Graham, Frank. *The Brooklyn Dodgers, An Informal History.* New York: G. P. Putnam's Sons, 1945, 1947, 1948.

Honig, Donald. *The Brooklyn Dodgers: An Illustrated Tribute.* New York: St. Martin's Press, 1981.

Schlossberg, Dan. *The Baseball Catalog.* Middle Village, N.Y.: Jonathan David Publishers, Inc., 1980.

Schoor, Gene. *The Complete Dodgers Record Book.* New York: Facts on File, 1984.

EDUCATION

Coulton, Thomas Evans. *A City College in Action: 1933–1958.* New York: Harper & Bros., 1955.

Gardner, Sara L. *Educational Corporations of New York State.* Albany: The University of the State of New York, 1924.

Gatner, Elliott S. M. "Long Island: The History of a Relevant and Responsive University 1926–1968." Ph.D. diss., Teachers College, Columbia University, 1974.

Horowitz, Murray M. *Brooklyn College: The First Half Century.* Brooklyn: Brooklyn College Press, 1981.

Kastendieck, Miles Merwin. *The Story of Poly.* Harvey Matthews and Co., 1940.

Nickerson, Marjorie L. *A Long Way Forward: The First Hundred Years of Packer Collegiate Institute.* Brooklyn: Packer Collegiate Institute, 1945.

FICTION

Aaronson, Sammy. *As High as My Heart.* New York, 1959.

Reznikoff, Charles. *Family Chronicle.* New York, the author, 1963.

Rosten, Norman. *Under the Boardwalk.* Englewood Cliffs, N.J.: Prentice-Hall, Inc., 1968.

Shulman, Irving. *The Amboy Dukes.* Garden City, N.Y.: Doubleday & Co., Inc., 1947.

Wolfe, Thomas. *Only the Dead Know Brooklyn.* Short stories. New York: The New American Library of World Literature, Inc., 1947.

GOVERNMENT SERVICES

Caro, Robert. *The Power Broker.* New York: Alfred A. Knopf, Inc., 1974.

Johnson, Gus. *F.D.N.Y.: 1900–1975.* Belmont, Mass.: Western Islands, 1977.

Mackeye, Milton. *The Tin Box Parade.* New York: Robert McBride and Co., 1934.

Rankin, Rebecca B., ed. *New York Advancing, 1934–35.* New York: Municipal Reference Library, 1936.

———. *New York Advancing: World's Fair Edition.* New York: Municipal Reference Library, 1939.

———. *New York Advancing: Victory Edition.* New York: Municipal Reference Library, 1945.

Triborough Bridge Authority. *Gowanus Improvement.* New York, 1941.

GROUP LIFE

Abelow, Samuel. *History of Brooklyn Jewry.* New York: Scheba Publishing Co., 1937.

Connolly, Harold X. *A Ghetto Grows in Brooklyn.* New York: NYU Press, 1977.

Federation of Jewish Philanthropies, Demographic Study Committee. *The Estimated Jewish Population of the New York Area, 1900–1975.* New York: the Federation, 1959.

Haick, Mary Ann. "The Syrian-Lebanese Community in South Ferry, Brooklyn, 1900–1922." Typescript pamphlet at Long Island Historical Society. Brooklyn, 1976.

Herling, Lillian. "A Study in Retardation with Special Emphasis on the Status of the Syrians." Master's thesis, Columbia University, 1929.

MacLeod, William Christie. *The Indians of Brooklyn in the Days of the Dutch.* New York: WPA Historical Records Survey, 1941.

Moore, Deborah Dash. *At Home in America: Second Generation New York Jews.* New York: Columbia University Press, 1981.

Rygg, A. N. *Norwegians in New York 1825–1925.* Brooklyn: The Norwegian News Co., 1942.

Welfare Council of the City of New York, Research Bureau. *Heads of Family by Color, Nativity, and Country of Birth.* New York: the Council, 1934.

Zenner, Walter P. "Syrian Jews in New York Twenty Years Ago," in V. Sauno, ed., *Fields of Offering.* Cranbury, N.J.: Associated University Presses, 1983.

NEIGHBORHOODS

Della Femina, Jerry, and Charles Sopkin. *An Italian Grows in Brooklyn.* Boston: Little, Brown and Co., 1978.

Hoffman, Jerome. *The Bay Ridge Chronicles.* Brooklyn: Bay Ridge Bicentennial Committee of Planning Board 10, 1976.

Ierardi, Eric J. *Gravesend: The Home of Coney Island.* New York: Vantage Press, Inc., 1975.

Israelowitz, Oscar. *Guide to Jewish New York City.* New York: the author, 1983.

Jewish Welfare Board. *Study of the Jewish Community of Williamsburg.* Unpublished. New York, 1936.

Kranzler, George. *Williamsburg: A Jewish Community in Transition.* New York: Philipp Feldheim, Inc., 1961.

Landesman, Alter F. *Brownsville.* New York: Bloch Publishing Co., 1969. Second edition, 1971.

———. *A History of New Lots, Brooklyn.* Port Washington, N.Y.: Kennikat Press, 1977.

Litchfield, Norman. "Blythebourne: A Community That Was Swallowed Up." *Journal of Long Island History,* Summer 1964.

Logan, Helen. *Williamsburg, A Neighborhood Study.* Unpublished. New York, 1940.

McCollough, Edo. *Good Old Coney Island.* New York: Charles Scribner's Sons, 1957.

Meyer, Egon. *From Suburb to Shtetl: The Jews of Boro Park.* Philadelphia: Temple University Press, 1979.

Philips, McCandlish. "Recollections of Coney Island," *The New York Times,* June 20, 1960.

Pilat, Oliver, and Jo Ranson. *Sodom by the Sea: An Affectionate History of Coney Island.* Garden City: Doubleday, Doran & Co., Inc., 1941.

Poster, William. " 'Twas a Dark Night in Brownsville." *Commentary,* September 1950.

Vosburgh, Walter S. *Racing in America 1866–1921.* New York: Priv. print 1922.

Willis, Houghton, and Charles Ditmas. *Flatbush: A Study in Transportation.* New York: 1920.

TRANSPORTATION

Cunningham, Joseph, and Leonard De Hart. *A History of the New York City Subway System.* 3 volumes. New York: the authors, 1977.

Fischler, Stanley I. *Moving Millions.* New York: Harper & Row, 1979.

Groh, Karl. "Above the Streets of Brooklyn." *ERA Headlights,* September–November 1975.

———. "Farewell to the 'R-9s.' " *ERA Headlights,* July–September 1977.

Kahn, Alan Paul, and Jack May. "Brooklyn Elevated Railroads, 1910." in *Tracks of New York.* New York: Electric Railroaders Association, 1975.

Rinke, Herman. "New York Subways: Fifty Years of Millions!" *Electric Railroads,* October 1954.

Watson, Edward B. "One Hundred Years of Street Railways in Brooklyn, 1854–1954." *ERA Headlights,* July 1954.

MISCELLANEOUS

Adams, Joey, with Henry Tobias. *The Borscht Belt.* New York: The Bobbs-Merrill Co., Inc., 1959.

Snyder, Robert. *This Is Henry, Henry Miller from Brooklyn.* Los Angeles; Nash Publishing Co., 1974.

Sutton, Willie, with Edward Linn. *Where the Money Was: The Memoirs of a Bank Robber.* New York: The Viking Press, 1976.

Turnbull, Andrew. *Thomas Wolfe.* New York: Charles Scribner's Sons., 1967.

Eastman, John. *Who Lived Where?* New York: Facts on File, 1983.

Glaubiger, Merel Pomerantz. *Hymie Schorenstein: A Political Biography.* New York, 1983.

Kazin, Alfred. *A Walker in the City.* New York: Harcourt, Brace & World, Inc., 1951.

Lapidus, Morris. *An Architecture of Joy.* Miami: E. A. Seemann Publishing, Inc., 1979.

Reynolds, Quentin. *I, Wilie Sutton.* New York: Farrar, Straus and Young, 1953.

INDEX